# A STUDENT'S GUIDE TO THE MELAB, 2ND EDITION

MARY C. SPAAN

Ann Arbor
THE UNIVERSITY OF MICHIGAN

Copyright © by the University of Michigan 1992, 2007, 2008
All rights reserved
ISBN 13: 978-0-472-03296-9
Published in the United States of America by
The University of Michigan Press
Manufactured in the United States of America
♾ Printed on acid-free paper

2011      2010      2009      2008          4    3    2    1

# PREFACE

I have been involved with English language testing since 1960. During that time I have scored, developed, written, constructed, pretested, and evaluated English as a Second Language (ESL) tests. Many who speak English as a second language have been my friends and colleagues as well as my students.

Many students of English are required to show that they can perform successfully as students in such fields as architecture, business, engineering, medicine, music, social work, etc. However, they are not sure of the proficiency level they should have reached in English to do this. Also, they are not sure what will be on the English test they are required to take.

These students wonder about the content of the Michigan English Language Assessment Battery (MELAB) test. They ask how to prepare for it. They are worried, and obviously what they need is a sample test to show them the format and difficulty level of the actual test, so that they can evaluate themselves.

Some of these students are proficient in English and should not worry about their performance on the test. They do not need more English instruction or practice, but they do need a self-assessment test and a model test to give them an idea of the content, the level of difficulty, and the testing method used in the MELAB. On the other hand, some students may have weaknesses of which they are not aware. They also need self-assessment so they can work to improve performance on their weak areas.

It is for all these students that I have written this book. I, and other test writers, want students to perform at their optimum—that is, do the best they can do—on our tests. We do not want students to get low scores just because they are not familiar with the test format or directions or have difficulty timing themselves. We hope students will familiarize themselves with these processes so that they can do their best. We don't want students to be afraid of the test. We want them to be familiar with its content and format and to be prepared.

This test book is not, therefore, designed to be memorized but to be studied as an approach to a certain kind of task or testing method. The best way to prepare for any test is to be competent (skilled and knowledgable) in the *subject matter*. The best way to study for the MELAB, or any other English language test, is to study English, rather than to study or memorize a test preparation book. Memorizing the sample tests in this book will not guarantee success on the MELAB or any other ESL test; studying and using English for reading, writing, listening, and speaking, over a long period of time, is the best way to become an expert user of English.

I wish to thank those who so generously supported me in this project: Sue Reinhart, who helped with the grammar commentaries; Joan Morley, who advised me on the listening portions, and her students, who critiqued the listening test; the two anonymous reviewers, for their insightful and substantive comments and suggestions on the preliminary manuscript; and my colleague Sarah Briggs and my husband David, who provided motivation and support.

# PREFACE TO THE 2ND EDITION

Since the first edition of this book was first published in 1992, several changes have taken place in both the content of the MELAB and in its administration. Most notable are changes to the Listening section, and the fact that much more information about the MELAB is now available on its website. Students, teachers, and MELAB administrators have asked that an updated version of this book be made available. I am pleased, therefore, to present this new edition.

Thanks go to Gary Buck, ELI-UM Testing Director, and John Swales, former ELI-UM Director, for their encouragement in this undertaking. I am especially grateful to two of my former colleagues in the ELI Testing Division: to Jeff Johnson, who provided me with materials and up-to-date information; and to Sarah Briggs, who critiqued the radio reports in the Listening section. We also gratefully acknowledge the voice talent of Pat Grimes, Badria Jazairi, and Kyle Norris.

# CONTENTS

# Introduction

## ■ WHAT IS THE MELAB?

The English Language Institute at the University of Michigan (ELI-UM) has made its English language proficiency testing services available to institutions of higher education (universities) as well as to businesses and government agencies for more than 50 years. The ELI-UM oversees the administration of the Michigan English Language Assessment Battery (MELAB), an advanced-level English language proficiency test designed to measure the English language ability of adult nonnative speakers of English who will need to use the language for academic purposes at the university level. The MELAB has also been used for screening job training and fellowship applicants.

The official MELAB is a secure test. This means the actual tests are not for sale, but they may be administered through the ELI-UM's testing service. Official MELAB tests are arranged through the ELI-UM and administered by official MELAB examiners in the United States and Canada. The examiners send test papers back to ELI-UM for scoring and reporting of scores.

The official MELAB consists of three parts; subscores on these components (parts) are averaged to produce the final score. These are scaled scores, not a number of correct responses to questions, and not a percentage score. (Scoring is explained further in Scoring and Interpreting Your Test on pages 127–31.) The components of the MELAB are:

Part 1: **Composition,** a 30-minute impromptu essay

Part 2: **Listening,** an audio multiple choice test measuring comprehension of spoken English

Part 3: **Grammar, Cloze, Vocabulary, Reading (GCVR),** an objective multiple choice test containing grammar, cloze reading, and vocabulary problems, and reading passages followed by comprehension questions.

An optional fourth part of the MELAB is a **speaking test** (oral interview) with the local examiner. The speaking test is required for some professional certification programs and for applicants to the University of Michigan. It is strongly recommended for applicants to graduate-level programs at U.S. universities who wish to be considered for graduate student teaching assistantships and for candidates for fellowships, grants, or job training programs.

The speaking test is not automatically included in every MELAB administration, but it cannot be taken separately from Parts 1, 2, and 3 of the MELAB. It is not offered at all MELAB test sites; contact the MELAB Office or go to the MELAB website **(www.lsa.umich.edu/eli/testing/melab/)** for information about MELAB Test Centers that offer the speaking test.

## ■ WHAT IS THE TESTING PROCEDURE?

You can get much detailed information about the MELAB from the English Language Institute. This includes a MELAB Information Bulletin, which contains a registration form, instructions, sample test, and list of current MELAB test centers. You may also contact the MELAB Office directly at:

English Language Institute
MELAB Office
University of Michigan
500 East Washington Street
Ann Arbor, MI 48104-2028  U.S.A.

Telephone: 1-866-MYMELAB
(Toll-free: 1-866-696.3522)
Fax: 734-615-6586
Email: **melabelium@umich.edu**
Website: **www.lsa.umich.edu/eli/testing/melab/**

To register for the MELAB, contact the test center of your choice (contact information is shown on the MELAB website under "Registration") to get information about test schedules, registration deadlines, and current test fees. You should mail your completed MELAB Official Identification Form, one passport photo, and test fee (see website or contact MELAB Office for current test fees) to the test center you have chosen. The test center will conduct the test, which takes about 2½ hours. The test center will send the completed test papers to ELI-UM for scoring and reporting.

**Eligibility:** you must wait a minimum of six weeks between each MELAB exam. You may take the MELAB only four times within any 12-month period.

**Special accommodations:** ELI-UM is committed to ensuring that every applicant be able to demonstrate his or her language ability under circumstances that are fair and that do not alter the construct (English language ability) being measured. For this reason, ELI-UM allows test applicants with disabilities to request special accommodations. This is to minimize the effect of the disability on test performance and to get the most accurate measure possible of the skill being tested. Contact the MELAB Office or see the website for information on types of disabilities that can be accommodated and on how to apply for special accommodations.

The MELAB Office will send you a copy of your score report. You may also authorize two official score reports at no extra charge. These score reports are for **schools** and/or **institutions only.** Your score report will show your separate scores on Parts 1, 2, 3, your speaking test score (if taken), and your final MELAB score (the average of Parts 1, 2, and 3). Your score report will also show descriptions and statistics of the different parts of the test.

## ■ HOW TO USE THIS BOOK

### Students

This book will help you in many ways:

1.  The unknown is always a little frightening. By becoming familiar with the content and layout of the MELAB, you will gain confidence in your ability to do well on the test. Model tests, which you may take for practice, follow. Take plenty of time to look at the examples, and read the instructions carefully before you begin each practice test. This will help you to understand the test format and to practice some of the basics before you begin the practice test. The practice tests are not taken from the official MELAB. However, they were written and edited by the same people who write the MELAB. Some of the test items have appeared in other ELI tests.

2.  You will get practice in following specific directions for taking this test. You should mark your answers to the Practice Test problems on one of the answer sheets in Appendix E.

3.  The MELAB will not only test your ability to use and recall written and spoken English, it will also test your fluency or speed in performing these tasks. The practice tests in this book will help you determine your speed. Before you begin a practice test, estimate how much quiet, uninterrupted time you will need to finish it, and then time yourself. (Take a watch or digital timer that does not beep with you to the actual MELAB if possible. Cell phones must be turned off.) Keep a record of how much time it took you to do each practice test. How much time did it take you? If it had been a real test, would you have finished within the time limit?

4.  Farther back in the book there is a scoring key for each practice test. For the listening tests, there is a script and a commentary about what you heard on the tape recording. For the GCVR practice tests, a commentary explains the answers to the problems. You will be able to score your practice test and review your answers to the problems to see why the correct answer is correct.

5.  After you score your practice test, you should go to the score interpretation section. You will be able to evaluate your performance on the test to get some idea of how you might do on the official MELAB. You will see your strengths and weaknesses.

**Reminder:** The best way to prepare for any test is to know the subject thoroughly, not just to concentrate on the testing method. Just memorizing the sample tests in this book will not guarantee you success on the MELAB or any other English test. It takes years of study and practice to become highly proficient in a foreign language.

## Teachers

The best way for students to prepare for the MELAB is to study and use a full range of English by reading widely, speaking with and listening to native speakers of English, and writing in English. They must practice English, not just memorize rules. Rules exist as helpful guidelines to explain why the language works the way it does.

It is important that this book be used as practice and familiarization for a certain kind of test, not as a "cram" book to be memorized. Memorization of this book will not by itself guarantee improved English language ability, nor will it guarantee improved performance on the MELAB. This book should not be used as the primary text for an ESL test preparation course. Rather, it should be considered supplemental to other textbooks that concentrate on the various skill areas to be measured.

If students have prepared well, they can be confident in their abilities, and they will not panic when it comes time to take a test. Taking a test is always a challenge; studying this book will ease the fear of the unknown for students taking the MELAB.

Test writers use a term called *task effect*. This means that the test method may affect a student's performance on a test. Sometimes a proficient student will not do well on a test because she or he did not follow the directions or was unfamiliar with the test method and format. A test preparation book such as this one should eliminate negative task effect and produce an optimal and valid performance.

Most teachers prefer to work on one skill area at a time. Therefore, you might want to spend a week or two on each of the three mandatory parts of the MELAB.

### Part 1

You might begin with timed impromptu essay writing. Begin by having your students write a timed 30-minute essay on their choice of two topics given in this book or on other topics of your choosing. Then, review their essays.

1. Did they follow instructions? Did they write on only one of the topics? Did they write on both? Did the essay address the topic, or did it seem "off topic"?

2. Were they able to write at least 150–200 words?

3. Look at clarity and accuracy of expression and ability to develop a theme with supporting argument and details (examples). Is the meaning clear? Does the organization help make the thoughts clear and easy to follow? Are your students

able to use complex as well as simple grammatical structures with a minimum of error? Do they use only simple sentence structures? Do they use a wide range of vocabulary appropriately? You may find it helpful to refer to the official MELAB composition descriptions and codes in Appendix B (page 135).

You could have students repeat this process several times, getting feedback from you after each essay. Students can be trained to spend one or two minutes organizing their thoughts, and possibly writing an outline, 20 to 25 minutes writing, then three or four minutes reviewing what they have written and making corrections, additions, or other changes.

## Part 2

Practice interactive speaking in class. Listen to both conversational dialogue and lecture recordings (both audio and video). Review the examples and instructions for the listening test carefully. Then review:

1. Did they follow instructions? Did they mark their answers only on the answer sheets? Did they mark in the test booklets? Make sure they don't make mistakes in mechanics during the "real" test.

2. Were they able to keep up with the speed of the recording? Some students understand something the first time they hear it, others can understand if the aural stimuli is repeated, and still others have difficulty even with repetition.

3. Encourage them to make a guess if they aren't sure of what they heard. For the official test, they won't be able to review their responses and what they think they heard, but for these practice tests, you could have them write what they thought they heard and then discuss this when reviewing the correct answers.

4. Some students don't take any notes at all during the lecture and radio report parts of the listening test. Some just have very good aural memory and don't seem to need to take notes about details, while others don't understand what they hear if it is in the form of longer discourse. Encourage your students to take notes, in outline form if possible, with some details. They should not write *everything* they hear, but note only the important points or details. This practice will aid them not only on the MELAB, but also in university-level coursework.

Check to see if errors occur more frequently in short utterance sections or in questions about longer discourse (the lecture and radio reports). Your students may need work on comprehending "fast speech," contractions, and idiomatic expressions. At lower proficiency levels, they may not be able to follow longer discourse (more than 20 seconds of continuous speech). At intermediate proficiency levels, they may understand the main idea of longer discourse but be unable to comprehend some of the details and how they relate to the main idea. Following the scoring of your students' tests, the audio recording can be replayed as they read the script so that the oral and written versions can be compared. You can help your students look for the main points of the lectures and radio reports as well as supporting details.

One useful source of different kinds of speech is the ELI-UM Michigan Corpus of Academic Spoken English (MiCASE). Sound files are available online, as are instructional materials for ESL/EAP teaching and for ESL self-study. The website is **www.lsa.umich.edu/eli/micase/**.

## Part 3

For Part 3, estimate percentages correct on each of the four sections. It may be that most of your students perform consistently on all sections of the test and just need general improvement and practice in all areas of the language. Others, however, may show relative strengths and weaknesses; for example, they may do well on reading but poorly on grammar, or vice versa. The commentaries following the answer keys can provide support for a review of the areas of weakness.

Before administering Practice Test 2, spend instructional time on each of the skill areas tested.

## Speaking Test

For the speaking test, students can practice interviewing each other, and taking part in classroom debates and discussions. They can be critiqued on intelligibility, interactiveness, and overall effectiveness by you, the teacher, as well as by each other (peer ratings).

# PRACTICE TESTS

# Part 1: Composition

This is a 30-minute impromptu (unprepared) essay. You are not allowed to use a dictionary or other notes or aids while writing it. The examiner will give you a form with instructions and two topics on it. (See Appendix A for a sample of this form.) You must write on *one* of the two topics. Do not try to write on both, and do not write about something else. If you write about something else, your paper will not be graded. If you do not understand the topics, ask the examiner to explain or translate them. Choose whichever topic is most interesting or appealing to you. Your choice will not make a difference in your score.

Make your topic choice quickly, then spend a minute or two planning your essay. If you wish, you may make an outline for your essay on the examination paper. You will not be graded on your outline; it is only to help you organize your thoughts. Once you begin writing, do not worry too much about minor errors you may have made; it is important that your writing be fluent (smooth-flowing) and not halting. When there are five minutes remaining, write a conclusion (ending or summary) to your essay. Then go back and edit it for additions, errors, or any other changes you wish to make. You may make these changes in the body of the essay, crossing out words and sub-stituting others.

Do not waste time copying your composition over so that it looks nice; you will not be graded on the appearance of your paper. You will not be graded on penmanship (handwriting), but try to write legibly, so the graders can read it.

It will help you to practice writing 30-minute essays, both for general practice in writing and for practice in writing within this time limit. The essay topics might ask you to narrate an experi-ence, to compare and contrast two things or ideas, to discuss the advantages and disadvantages of something, or possibly to take a position on a topic (have an opinion) and defend it (explain why you believe it, giving examples). Here are some examples of topics that have been used in the past:

1. What is the funniest thing that ever happened to you? Describe.
2. Would you raise your children the same way your parents raised you? Why or why not? Explain and give examples.
3. How should students be evaluated: according to their achievements or their effort? Discuss.
4. What do you think is the biggest environmental problem in your country? Explain in detail and tell what you think can be done to solve it.
5. What public figure, living or dead, do you admire most? Why?

6.   What are the characteristics of a good teacher? Explain and give examples.

7.   What are the problems of a student who wishes to study in a foreign country? Discuss university admissions, passport, visa, language problems, etc.

8.   If you could give the President of the United States advice on improving relations with your country, what would you tell him or her?

9.   Would you prefer to live in a large city or in the country (rural area)? Explain the reasons for your choice.

10.   In your opinion, what are the causes of divorce? What do you think are the greatest problems caused by divorce?

11.   For men: imagine that you were born a woman. How would your life be different? For women: imagine that you were born a man. How would your life be different? Explain and give examples.

12.   If there were a country that was the single source of a major resource, would that country have the right not to share the resource with other countries? Why or why not?

13.    If you could be another person for one day, who would you be, and how would you spend the time?

14.   What advice would you give someone who wants to learn English?

15.   Imagine that you are in charge of establishing the first colony on the moon. What kind of people would you choose to take with you? What qualities and technical skills should they have?

16.   What are the effects of modern technology on the way of life in your country?

Remember, these are just examples of past topics, and they will *not* appear on your test. Do not try to memorize and write a composition on one of these topics when you take the MELAB.

All MELAB essays are graded at the English Language Institute at the University of Michigan. When assigning scores, the raters consider development of ideas or theme, organization and connection of ideas, fluency and clarity of expression, ability to use a variety of simple and complex syntactic structures, range and appropriateness of vocabulary, and ability to express things in detail and give good examples.

Compositions that contain only very short, simple sentences and simple vocabulary cannot be given the highest scores. If errors are not frequent and if they do not confuse your meaning, they will not lower your score much.

Each essay is read by at least two trained raters who do not know each other's scores. If there is a great difference in the scores assigned the essay, a third rater will also score it. Reading is done holistically (a single overall score is given, rather than separate ratings for different things). Grades are assigned on a ten-point scale, with scores ranging from 97 to 53. Possible scores are 97, 93, 87, 83, 77, 73, 67, 63, 57, 53. If the graders assign two scores that are close to each other on the scale, an average score will be reported. For example, one score of 87 and the other of 83 will be reported as an 85. In addition, a letter code might be assigned. Letter codes show features of your writing that the graders thought were especially strong or weak in relation to the overall level of your writing. Appendix B lists the official MELAB composition numerical descriptions and letter codes.

## ■ SAMPLE ESSAYS

Some essays written by actual MELAB examinees follow. Before each essay, the score and a general description of what it represents are given. Following each essay is a discussion of the features that determined the raters' score.

## Essay 1

*Score 97*

Very full, clear development of theme. Fluent, complex, broad vocabulary, error-free. Similar to well-educated adult native speaker of English who is also a good writer.

**Topic:** People who have been seriously injured can be kept alive by machines. Do you think they should be kept alive at great expense, or allowed to die?

1   There has been a lot of publicity recently about whether a person should be kept alive by
2   machines or allowed to die. This controversial question has generated a lot of debate; on
3   one hand, there are people who say that a person must be kept alive by any means because
4   no one has the right to decide whether a person should live or die, while on the other hand,
5   there are people who think that such a seriously injured person should be allowed to die
6   and not be kept dependent on a machine for the rest of his or her life because allowing
7   that person to die is more merciful.
8      Personally, I think that in certain cases where the patients are in great suffering then it
9   is more merciful to let the patient die in dignity. If there is no way that a patient will ever
10   recover and live independently of the machine then it would be kinder to let the patient die.
11   The Pro-Life group of people would argue that with so much research going on there might
12   one day be a cure for these patients and we shouldn't allow them to die. Of course, such
13   a cure might be found but could the patient's relatives bear to see the suffering of the
14   patient, living like a vegetable? I believe that if the patient is in a sound mind and able to
15   make his own decision then the patient himself should be allowed to say whether he wants
16   to live or die, otherwise it is his close relative who should make the decision.
17      In cases where there is a very good chance that the patient will recover and does not
18   have to be dependent on the machine to be alive then it should be clear that he be allowed
19   to live. It can be also that the patient expresses a desire to live even though heavily
20   dependent on the machine; then of course, his wishes should be respected.

21     I think that it is a very sorry thing to keep hanging on to life attached to a machine for

22 the rest of one's life. After all, life is only worth living if one can live it with dignity, to face

23 each day with a challenge. Although I've never been in such a situation, I can feel what it

24 is like to be dependent on a machine for the rest of one's life. I don't think the expense of

25 keeping such a person alive should be the issue—the issue should be "are we doing the

26 right thing keeping that person alive?" or "are we doing the right thing letting him die?"

27     In conclusion, I think the best thing to do is that each case should be reviewed closely.

28 If there's really no hope whatsoever of the patient recovering then it is more merciful to let

29 him die unless he expresses a desire to live; then his wishes should be respected. Deciding

30 whether a person should live or die is not easy—it is like taking on the work of God.

**Comments:** Full, complete development of argument; can see both sides of the problem; gives plenty of supporting details. Organization and development are good: Para. 1 restates both sides of the problem, without reusing the words of the prompt (assigned topic); Para. 2 gives the circumstances under which one choice would be preferable, and the writer includes counter arguments (examples of arguments against the writer's opinion); Para. 3 gives the circumstances under which a different choice would be preferable; Para. 4 returns to a rephrasing of the opinions expressed in Para. 2; and Para. 5 summarizes the writer's position: to look at the specific circumstances of each situation before making a decision.

    Fluent writing shows excellent range and control of grammar and vocabulary. Complex syntactic structures are used successfully: Lines 2–3 *on one hand* ties into Line 4 *while on the other hand*; Line 17 *in cases where* is followed by Line 18 *then it should be clear*. Extensive embedding is used: Line 5 *there are people who think*; Lines 23–24 *I can feel what it is like to be*. Good use of hypotheticals (*if* clauses): Lines 9, 14, 22, 28; and modals: Lines 1 (*should*), 3 (*must*), 5 (*should*), 13 (*might*), etc. Vocabulary is broad and used appropriately: Line 2 *controversial, generated*, Line 2 *debate*, Line 9 *dignity*, Line 10 *recover*, Line 19 *expresses a desire*, Line 20 *wishes should be respected*, Line 21 *a very sorry thing*, Line 28 *recovering*.

## Essay 2

*Score: 93*

Full, clear development of theme. Fluent, complex, good vocabulary range. Should be as good as a native-speaker university student who does not have writing problems. Errors are few, sometimes native-type errors. Sometimes articles, or occasionally a preposition, sound "foreign" but do not hinder a reader's comprehension.

**Topic:** People who have been seriously injured, etc.

1     The basic issue involved here concerns human rights and more specifically, the right to

2 live. One has sole right to decide on his life, whether he wishes to live or to terminate his

3   'miserable' life, provided he is considered normal enough, i.e. he is not insane or suffering from
4   any disease which could obstruct human reasoning. In the movie "Whose life is it anyway?"
5   a paralysed man fought for his right to die but only after proven perfectly capable of
6   making a reasonable decisions as a human being. However, when a victim is not consciously
7   aware of himself or herself, then someone else must make a decision. But who?
8       It all depends on whether the involved party has provided any instructions as to what
9   is to be done in case of such an emergency. Although this itself seemed highly unlikely,
10  it does seem sufficiently practical a solution to problems of similar nature! Perhaps
11  everyone should make it a rule to take such a precaution. Anyway the real controversy is
12  still unsolved yet.
13      Suppose a person is in an unconscious state of mind, maybe in a coma etc., and incapable
14  of decision-making while not 'saying' in advance in some selfpredetermined manner his (or
15  her) "final" wishes. Then it would be most appropriate to gather all parties close to the
16  victim (but only those who have a concrete idea of how the victim would have decided, viz.
17  spouse, parents and close friends) for a poll, a vote to make the decision.
18      Otherwise let the jury decide it in court!

**Comments:** Good development of one side of the issue; might provide more general background in introduction. Good syntactic range: Line 2 *whether he wishes to live or to terminate,* Lines 8–9, *depends on whether . . . as to what is to be done in case of,* Line 14, *while not saying.* Good control, only occasional errors which are not distracting: Line 2 article deletion, *one has sole right,* Line 6 lack of agreement, *a reasonable decisions.* Uses high-level, sophisticated vocabulary: Line 2, *terminate,* Line 5, *paralysed,* Line 10, *sufficiently,* Line 11, *precaution.*

## Essay 3

*Score 87*

Full, clear development of theme. Meaning is clear; writing is fluent. Usually clearly organized; discourse-level and sentence-level syntax (grammatical structures) are good. Occasional article or preposition misuse or awkward phrase makes it obvious that the writer is a not native.

**Topic:** Discuss the advantages and disadvantages of having a part-time job instead of a full-time job.

1   For many people, holding a part-time job is terrible and unthinkable because they  think
2   of its disadvantages only. To my mind, a part-time job offers disadvantages as well as
3   advantages.
4       The most valuable thing in life is time—it can not be bought. A part-time job allows
5   you much spare time for you to engage in other activities, important or unimportant but
6   necessary. If you are interested in writing, for example, you can write a lot during your

7   spare time, and one day in the future you may succeed. You can also study a lot if you
8   want; if you want to be a composer, you may have adequate time to make music. Anyway,
9   a part-time job will allow you some kind of concentration on doing what you want to, while
10  as a full-time job will keep you busy and tired—after you come home after work, you are
11  likely to have need of rest, then you can do little during the very limited spare time. Again,
12  because you work less hours for you part-time job, you won't feel so tired and bored with
13  your work. And you may have a variety of activities in your life. However, a full-time job will
14  keep you confined to the workshop, if you're a worker, and you will become some sort of
15  a machine yourself. Men, after all, are not machines; they need something more besides
16  making money by working.
17      However, a part-time job doesn't make you earn much money which is needed for daily
18  necessities. Money sometimes allows you more freedom in your life. And, if you have a
19  family to support, it's inappropriate to have a part-time job only. You will feel you're hard
20  up for money and that will perhaps affect your activities which might lead to future
21  success. Again, you don't have a job security if you have a part-time job, and this may
22  cause you worries. Anyway, for a person from a rich family, a part-time job is excellent; for
23  a poor person, it is not.

**Comments:** Well organized around a unifying principle (time is valuable, therefore a part-time job is good because it allows you more time); includes another point of view in Para. 3 (disadvantages of lack of money, job security).

Sometimes awkwardly expressed: in Lines 2–3, the writer should put *advantages* before *disadvantages* to express his/her view to contrast with that of the *many people* who *think of disadvantages only* (Lines 1–2); Line 12, *work . . . **for you** part-time job* could be corrected to ***at your** part-time job*; Line 21 uses an unnecessary article, ***a** job security*. Such errors of preposition choice and article use often appear at advanced proficiency levels. In general, though, the writing appears natural and fluent, and broad vocabulary is shown: Line 8, *adequate,* Line 9, *concentration,* Lines 17–18, *daily necessities.*

## Essay 4

*Score: 83*

Clear development of theme. Meaning is clear; writing is fluent. Variety of syntactic (sentence-level grammatical) structures used well, localized errors less numerous than at the 77 level. Transitions may not always be clearly indicated or smoothly achieved. Some, but not all of these characteristics may be present (i.e., errors take on an idiosyncratic character): vocabulary is basic, lacking specificity; there might be problems with prepositions, articles, some pronouns.

**Topic:** People who have been seriously injured, etc.

1   First of all, the point isn't the expense at all. We are lucky to live in a sociaty where money
2   can't be more important than keeping someone alive. However the matter is much more
3   difficult but in some other aspect. When someone is seriously injured and then being kept
4   alive by some machines, it's very important for me to know, whether or not the patient is
5   conscious. If he/she is conscious, according to my opinion, he/she must be kept alive even
6   by machines. As long you can still think, as long you can still improve in your soul. You must
7   be given the chance to live longer as long as it's possible—I would like to emphasize once
8   more than expenses may not count at all—If you've became unconscious, and supposed
9   you'll remain like that, the matter turns to be much deeper, and much more difficult.
10  According to the laws what all the doctors have to follow they will keep you alive. The question
11  overshows upon duty. The point is whether or not they have the right for doing so or they
12  don't. This has been discussed for a long time and everybody has his individual opinion about
13  it. I, personally was working in several hospitals. I was a male nurse, an operating assistant,
14  ambulance attendant, I have been working with sick people for over four years. I've very
15  much experience, I was listening to diing people, I've heard lots of very interesting opinion
16  according to the matter, we are discussing now. And none of those opinions were the same.
17  The only resemblance was that you can choose from two answers "yes" or "no." But the
18  individual way on what these people tried to approach the question, didn't even resemble
19  one another. Once a man who was suffering with cancer and had only a few days left told
20  me that he wouldn't agree, supposed his condition would turn even to worse, with keeping
21  him alive by using any machines because he thinks that he has the right—maybe the last
22  one—to choose from suffering longer, or diing in peace. I can't blame him. Once you get into
23  a situation, and we all have to chance to get there, what would you choose?
24     Well, this is one of the most difficult problem what many people were triing to solve, but
25  without result. This is a problem what can be solved only individually, thereby everyone will
26  come to his own conclusion. And, whatever that conclusion would be, we all have to respect
27  each an every answer, each and every solution.
28     The answers can depend on several factors. Eg. if the person is religious, he might say.
29  before. I, Although I suffer, I don't have to decide about my lif, what my God has given to me."

**Comments:** The argument is developed fairly fully, and there is good use of detail (the writer draws from his/her experience in hospitals, Lines 13–16, 19–22), but the organization isn't always clear, and the writer doesn't use enough paragraph markers. It could be improved by restating the problem at the beginning of the essay, rather than immediately starting with examples (Lines 1, 3–5). There is good use of complex structures, though some errors occur at the local level. For example: lack of parallelism in Sentence 3, Lines 2–3; incorrect choice of relative pronoun in Line 10, *what* for *that* or *which*; problems with word choice, Line 11, *overshows*, Line 20, *turn* rather than *become*; Lines 13–16, run-on sentence. Occasional spelling errors are not serious because they do not cause misunderstanding: Line 1, *sociaty*, Line 29, *lif*.

## Essay 5

*Another Example of an "83" Essay*

**Topic:** Imagine you are in charge of establishing the first colony on the moon. What kind of people would you choose to take with you? What qualities and technical skills should they have?

1    If I were to in charge of establishing the first colony on the moon, I will not be too picky
2    about the characters of the people who I am going to take with me, but rather I demand
3    them to be enthusiastic about their lifes. Also, each of them should at least have some
4    skills in order to contribute in making a better land and society.
5       It is important for me to choose only those that are enthusiastic about their lifes
6    because I think these people will be willing to work hard and will set an aim to their lifes. It
7    is also because to establish a new colony requires hard working people. Those who always
8    like to eat and sleep just will not help.
9       Besides being enthusiastic, the people I will take with me must know some technical
10   skills. Doctors are the first on my list for I donot know conditions but there on the moon,
11   there may be diseases and my people may get affected. I will also bring with me builders and
12   architects to help to build houses, roads, hospitals etc. Professors and school teachers will
13   also be on my list for I will not want our next generation to be illiterate. Also, I will bring some
14   good cooks, and some dress-makers, in order to allow my colony to be more modernized.
15   Mechanics and technicians will also be on my lists to help make light, electricity, etc.

**Comments:** Clearly addresses the topic (Para. 1 states that the writer wants enthusiasm and technical skills rather than character, Para. 2 discusses enthusiasm, and Para. 3 discusses technical skills) but lacks detail and full development. No summation is given at the end. There is fairly good control of grammar and vocabulary (Line 9, *Besides being enthusiastic*), with occasional minor errors (Line 3, *lifes* [lives], Line 4, *contribute **in*** [toward] *making*, Lines 9–10, ***know*** [have] *technical skills*).

## Essay 6

*Score: 77*

The theme is clearly but not always fully developed. The writing is basically understandable and fluent. The writer knows and uses complex syntax (sentence-level grammar), but not without fairly frequent discrete morphological (localized) errors, *or* the writer may use only a limited syntactic range. There may be verb tense problems and confusion between use of active and passive voice. The vocabulary is usually appropriate or a reasonable substitute for a more appropriate word, but may not always be highly specific. Often lacks discourse-level connectors (such as *because, since, nevertheless, moreover*).

**Topic:** People who have been seriously injured, etc.

1    Every human being has the right to live since they were to be born in this world. Nobody
2    has the right to end their life just because they were coma, or could not be process
3    anymore. In my opinion, I would say they should be kept alive, but also it depends on
4    certain circumstances such as the most important thing is financial background, also
5    the age of the patient.
6       Of course, a person who is going to spend most of his or her life on bed at the hospital
7    and with a lots of help from doctor, nurses and also machine to keep him alive, it certainly
8    need a large sum of money. If the victim came from a wealthy family and still young, his
9    family should let him live because with all the efforts from doctors and medicine, probably
10    after few months or few years later there is a changes for him to reborn again. If the
11    victim is old, it is really a sad thing for him to suffer in the hospital. Death probably is
12    the best way for him to go. However, if the victim came from a poor family background,
13    his or her parents couldn't afford his hospital fees, mostly his has to end his life for the
14    beneficial of his family.
15       However, letting a person who is not really dead to die is a cruel thing to do. To certain
16    people, they prefer to die rather than spending their whole life in the hospital and hoping
17    for mysterious to come.

**Comments:** Good development of argument and tries to show several points of view. Good attempts at simple and complex syntax with subordination: Lines 3–4, *I would say they should be . . . but also it depends on.* However, there are frequent localized errors: Line 2, *process*; Line 6, *on bed*; Line 7, *a lots of help*; Lines 7–8, *it certainly need*; Line 10, *changes*; Line 14, *beneficial.* The overall syntax breaks down in Para. 1, Lines 3–5, and Para. 2, Lines 8–10. Sometimes the errors cause lack of clarity and confusion in meaning: Lines 16–17, *hoping for mysterious to come.*

## Essay 7

*Another "77" Essay*

**Topic:** People who have been seriously injured, etc.

1    The most horoble thing for someone would be to loose or injure a part from his or her
2    body. Such kind of people feel that the're missing something, there's something wrong with
3    them or they even go farther and think that they're worthless and useless. If the most
4    weight is on psychological problems then there ussualy can be found an answer. Social
5    workers, the family enviroment do their best.
6       The most difficult problems that we face are when a person has to stay all lifelong
7    becide or by the influence of some machine. What do we do? Let him live or help him die? My
8    personal opinion on this matter is let him live, No matter what it costs. There is a life we're

9    dealing with. That person has the right to live. But my question-statement: Everything we

10   think of people, is money? We should also keep them alive, because there could be a chance

11   that with the progress of Sciense, a cure may be found for that certain disease.

12        Anyway we have an army of Scientists which are trying to find anything that can be

13   found; helpfull and destroyfull.

14        We have no right to allow someone to die unless he requests it. When the casualty is

15   consious and communicates and is able to understand and be understoud, and also speak

16   for himself then we should leave it up to him. He decides whether he wants to live under

17   those conditions, or he preffer diying than suffering and being a problem to others.

18        Because we ussually think and treat these people as a problem. The're not problems. We

19   could be in their case any time. Why are we called humans for? Letting our fellow people to

20   die because the cost or make our life a little uncomfortable?

21        The earn to live.

**Comments:** Fairly good command of structures, but breaks down in spots, and the meaning is unclear, especially in the last two paragraphs. The writer tends to use simple syntactic structures. The choice of transition or summary words (discourse markers) is not always good: Line 12, *Anyway*. There are some problems with word choice: Line 14, *casualty*; and word form: Line 2, *the're*; Line 13, *destroyfull*. Spelling errors are frequent and distracting but don't cause a breakdown in communication: Line 1, *horoble*, Line 4, *ussually*, Line 5, *enviroment*, Line 11, *Science*, Line 15, *consious*, Line 17, *diying*.

## Essay 8

*Score: 73*

Theme not always fully developed; transitions might be incomplete or unclear. Understandable without too much effort by the reader. Fluent in spots, but not necessarily throughout. Simple sentence structures are successful, and attempts at complex structures are made with some success. Many discrete (local) errors. Problems occur with pronouns, relative clauses, sentence fragments, and verbals. Basic vocabulary is usually adequate, but lacks highly specific words.

**Topic:** Part-time instead of full-time job.

1    A part-time job has been getting popular recently. Not only the college students have a

2    part-time job, but also the housewives have a part-time job. Now, what are the advantage

3    and the disadvantage points about a part-time job?

4         First, I want to discuss about the advantage points. As for the college students, it is

5    good for them to get a part time job, because they get some money so that they can enjoy

6    their hobbies or save money. Furthermore, Having part-time-job is very good experience for

7    them, because they understand how difficult they get money by themselves. As for the

8 housewives, though they work in order to get better domestic economic, that is also good
9 for them to understand value of money.
10     Second, the disadvantage point of a part-time job; for example, the college students
11 who have their part-time job don't have time to study. That is the problem. And the
12 housewives who have their part-time job don't have time to take care of their children and
13 do their houseworks.
14     As a result, a part-time job is good for getting money, but affect on time.

**Comments:** This is well organized and clear but shows limited development and language. The organization is very clear: Para. 1 states the popularity of part-time jobs for students and housewives, then asks the rhetorical question about the advantages and disadvantages; Para. 2 describes some advantages for both students and housewives; Para. 3 describes some disadvantages, again for both students and housewives; and Para. 4 is a one-sentence summary. However, the theme is not fully developed, and the essay is very short. The writer does not elaborate (explain in detail). While transition markers such as *First* (Line 4) and *Second* (Line 10) are clear and help show organization, they are not as sophisticated as other markers (such as *Initially, Furthermore, However, on the other hand*) or transition sentences would be. The syntax and vocabulary are also somewhat limited and simple, though the meaning is clear.

## Essay 9

*Another "73" Essay*

**Topic:** People who have been seriously injured, etc.

1 Many things may happen to the people during their lives, and many injuries may come to them.
2 Also many children are born with many kindes of deseaces. Scientists are studying whether
3 to let these people to live as normal people or to getride of them by sending them to death.
4 I think people who have been seriously injured and children who have been born with serious
5 gentic deseaces, must have the right to live there own lives, and there is no choise for
6 doctors or nay others people to end an injured men'slives. People should be kept alive, even
7 though it coast s agreat deal of maney. If doctors said the people who injured allowed to
8 die, he would interfer in the business of God. Because God only can end Man's life.
9 The governments are sepending many to creat wars. Then after the wars end, there must
10 be many people who injoured during the war, therefore, governments oughts to spend
11 money for the victims of the wars. The governments must take care of those injured
12 people during the war.
13 And about children who were born with gentic deseaces the have the right to live and no
14 one can end their lives, because they were born in these condition for aporpos. God wants
15 to sea and examin the one who will be patient and strong facing the problems. And God
16 wants to reward these perons for his patience.

17  Finally the injured person also can't end his life for being injured because thise is the
18  life. One must face the problems and the meserable life very strongly and firmly. And
19  the governments should spend alot of many to make those men feel better and live
20  abetter life—Because the govermments are fit first resporsible for there injury. The
21  Governmentscreat the proplems and the public afford the effects.

**Comments:** This is more fluent than the other "73" essay, and it uses more complex structures, but it has many more errors. The theme shows some development, and begins well by naming two types of ill people: those who have been injured and those who were born with diseases. The transitions and organization are not always clear, and lack of paragraph indentations makes it somewhat difficult to follow: Para. 2 (Lines 4–8) apparently concerns people with genetic diseases; then Para. 3 (Lines 9–12) at first appears unrelated, but eventually returns to injured people; and finally Para. 4 (Lines 13–16) unexpectedly returns to people with genetic diseases. The logic of Para. 5 (lines 17–21) is not always clearly explained (why is the government responsible?). The writing is fairly fluent and attempts complex syntax (Lines 2–3, 4–6, 6–7), though there are run-on sentences and sentence fragments (Lines 8, 13–14). Spelling and punctuation are poor, causing some confusion in meaning: Line 3, *getride*, Line 14, *aporpos*. Usually "73" essays will have better spelling and punctuation than this. Because of a combination of grammar, vocabulary, and spelling errors, some phrases are very difficult to understand: Lines 17–18, *because thise is the life*; Line 20, *the governments are fit first resporsible*; Line 21, *the public afford the effects*.

## Essay 10

*Score: 67*

Theme is not fully developed; transitions are incomplete or unclear. Understandable, but only with some effort by the reader; fluency is lacking. Most simple sentences are successful, but errors occur in attempts at complex structures. One particular syntactic (grammatical) structure may be used throughout. Many errors of all sorts.

**Topic:** Moon colony.

1  If I were in charge of establishing the first colony on the moon, I would take my husband, a
2  doctor, a nurse and a artchiteture.
3    If I wanted to create a new world, I should create humans If I did not bring my husband
4  with. How could I create humans? There was no people on the moon for even.
5    If the humans were create on the moon, it was improtant for them to have a medicine
6  care. Everyone would be sick at any time. When they are sick, they have to consult a
7  doctor. It was improtant for me to bring a doctor and a nurse. It was because I wanted
8  to create the human. If I gave birth, no people knew how to take care of me. If I died, who
9  would create the human on the moon?

10   I lived on the moon. There is a lot of space. I could built a big house. Thus, I could live
11   comfortably. Hence, I needed to bring a artchiteture. The artchiteture would design a
12   suitable house for me.
13     When I were in change of world, I would need electronic skill. Even on the moon, It has
14   a day and night. During a night time, it is very dark. I could not do anything. I needed a
15   light. If I did not have electronic skill, I would not have a light for even. All the thing I could
16   is sleep during the night.
17     Also, I could bring a plane Although I created the human on the moon, I had to go back
18   to the earth to visit my family. It was convinence for me to visit them if I had plane. I could
19   go back every time I liked.
20     I had to bring the cooking skills. Although I lived in the moon. It didn't means I did not
21   need to eat anything I ate food in order to have energy. If I did not know how to cook, I
22   just would drink some water and eat the raw food for even. Hence, I would died very soon.
23   Therefore, cooking skills were improtant for me.

**Comments:** Basically, limited with many errors. This is a rather low 67 because the structures used are so basic and limited. No overall organizing principle is given. The organization begins adequately but then breaks down. There are no transitions between paragraphs, and no hierarchy (ordering from most important to least important) of ideas is present. Para. 1 begins with people to bring to the colony, and lists husband, doctor, nurse, and *artchiteture* (architect). Then Para. 2 briefly explains the necessity of the husband, Para. 3 that of the doctor and nurse, and Para. 4 that of the architect. After this, the organization becomes unclear and seems to be only a list of ideas. Structurally, there are many simple sentences (Lines 10, 14–15, 20). The writer lacks control of complex structures, and there are many verb tense problems, especially with hypotheticals (*if* clauses) and modals. Lines 1–2 show successful use of the hypothetical, but in Line 7 the wrong verb is used (*was improtant* rather than *would be*), in Line 3 the wrong modal is used (*should* rather than *would* or *would have to*), and in Line 8 the wrong verb is used again (*if I gave birth, no people knew*, rather than *would know*.) Spelling errors are distracting, and sometimes slow the reader (Lines 15 and 22, *even* instead of *ever*).

# Essay 11

*Another "67" Essay*

**Topic:** People who have been seriously injured, etc.

1   The medicine in the world is preceeding quickly and the purpose of that is only to protect
2   the human-being, and in the same time we cann't evaluate the human being by money, and
3   I know that the machines designed for keeping the people who injured or any thing else
4   alive. In my opinion if I have to choose between paying a lot of money to save a person or
5   leave him die I,ll choose the first one, just for one reasen because if the person works he
6   can get money but its imposible to create a person by the machines.

7    In the other way if the person who injured cann't pay to save himself The governument
8    of his country has to take care of these problems because in any way The hospitals who
9    take care of these persons has a lot of expenses for that htis problem has to be solved
10   already by high responsibles or governors, because the human being has to stay the most
11   important thing in this life.
12   There is another thing the people can do it to establish or to create a big associations
13   to take care of the poor people and to handle them with a kid gloves because all times
14   they need helping and surrerting from the high class of people.

**Comments:** This writer tries more complex language, but the writing is error-ridden. The argument is not always clear, especially in Para. 2, Lines 7–11, regarding the explanation of why the government should pay. There are some problems with logic, as in Lines 5 and 6, where the connection between machines and money is not clear. There are problems with sentence structure: run-on sentences appear in Lines 4–6 and Para. 2, Lines 7–11. A sentence fragment appears in Lines 3–4. Subordination is not always successful or is not used where it should be (Line 9). There are some inappropriate lexical (word choice) problems: Line 7, *In the other way,* rather than *on the other hand;* and Line 10 *responsibles* for *authorities;* one lexical item is incomprehensible: Line 14, *surrerting.* Nonetheless, some use of high-level vocabulary is shown: Line 1, *preceeding* [proceeding], Line 2, *evaluate.*

# Essay 12

*Another "67" Essay*

**Topic:** Moon colony.

1    The kind of peiple to be choosen would be, the ones that in one way or another hard show
2    How weel, and Responsably they are. go to the moon is a factor of behaverr and the people
3    that is going to enjoy that colony have to have not just good actituds but also education
4    and be able get command.
5    They wiil be able to remaind calm by the time it may would be reguaire they will need to
6    have a high level in any kind of technical skills and those may be, computer, food, ecology
7    etc. this people will be the ones to live in there, will be no Rivers, walks in the park or anything
8    like that, so they would need to be prepare mentally and fisically to this new experience. No
9    body is going to help them, becouse they would be far away from they original planet, also
10   they will need to live as one becouse lonliness may be a factor.
11   Establishing a new colony in the moom maigh take a cople years but by the time it come
12   we will be rady becouse since now, education is been giving, and young people are the gnes
13   in the way of learning. The future is greate and so is the aportuinity, our future knites
14   of the mood will be the first step forward to gain the space, and travel arround the hold
15   universe will be like go for a Ride in one sundy morning.

16   The futur aritauts of the moon will be the ones to get the will of the human Race, and
17   theryore they are goinng to be blacks, chineses, Spanish etc people for all arraind the
18   world, will enjoy this cruse, with the jope of create love, respect, and confidence in every
19   one of them, ones againg, they wil need to work as a group in order to survive, and put all
20   their technical skills together in order to make so anelate gold.

**Comments:** The writer attempts complex structures and phrases but with many errors: Lines 11–13 show good overall structure but have frequent localized errors. Some inappropriate word choice is shown: Line 1, *hard*, Line 2, *factor*, Line 12, *giving*. Some incorrect word forms are used: Line 2, *Responsably*. The frequent spelling errors are distracting and tend to impede comprehension because of their frequency and severity: Line 2, *weel*, Line 3, *actituds*, Line 5, *reguaire*, Line 11, *maigh*, Line 16, *aritauts*, Line 17, *arraind*.

## Essay 13

*Score: 63*

Theme undeveloped, unclear. Sometimes short. May be difficult to understand. Has control over some simple sentences and limited vocabulary.

**Topic:** Moon colony.

1   First that all, I need The perfect conditions for your lives. This conditions are for example:
2   houses, stores, medical center and other places, but for this places is neccessary their
3   construction. I need people with this technical, equipment and people ables in enroller this
4   group, this people are youngers and with a good capacity for to do your work.
5   In other words, I need people with experience in give and reciber orders.
6   When the construction is finished with the places readys I need people of each profession
7   of both sexs for your completion and necesary.
8   All the places will have a good conditions for comfort the each person and all people
9   will have theirselves satisfaction. In this colony will have a lot communications, because
10   whole people will be friendly, and generous.
11   This communications are for example: radio, TV, telephone, and a lot roads.
12   In the comfort, they will have restaurant,. place for enjoy, for example parks, disck and
13   other places.
14   The economic in my colony is very cheap, because the foot was around of the agriculture.
15   The people will use the sun for the electricity and the water for evaporation of lage and
16   then a recicle.
17   All of the waste willbe procces and recicle.
18   All them leaving in peace.

**Comments:** Lacks an overall organizing principle; mostly lists with no dominant theme. Frequently confusing to the reader. Communication would have been improved if the writer had indented paragraphs, thus helping signal transitions to the reader. Some conditions of living on the moon are given: Para. 4, houses and comfort, Para. 5, communications, Para. 6, restaurant, Para. 7, economy (not explained), and Para. 8, power source. However, none are tied together under any organizing idea or theme. Short sentence structures are fairly successful, but many words are out of order (e.g., Lines 8–9). Frequently the wrong word form is used: Line 12, *enjoy*, Line 14, *economic*. Word choices are not used well: Line 1, *that*, Line 10, *whole people*. Pronouns are used incorrectly in a way that confuses the reader: *your* in Lines 1, 4, and 7.

## Essay 14

*Another "63" Essay*

**Topic:** People who have been seriously injured, etc.

1   Poeple come to leaf to live, for this reason we should try as hard as possible to keep them
2   alive. If we sign dwon to allowed them to die, this mistake we will never forget. In my opoin,
3   to take part in dision of allowing someone to death, even if her or she seriously injured, is
4   the same as to kill someone in a good health. These machines which the human event it
5   should take part in saving the other leafs.
6   We might be mean for a person or other, but being mean in saving someone leaf is a crime.
7   Why we have to store our money in banks although we all know that the money come and
8   go and no one can be sure that his money will remain with him until he die.
9   In case I do not have any money,and in the same time my borther or sister or any one
10  of my relative is suffering from his serious enjured do I have to watch or allowed him to
11  die? even though I have a good reeson to allowed him to die I won't do it. I might work in
12  another jobe beside mine, ask friends for help ask any bank or organization for lending me
13  the money I need.
14  I have to do my duty in the best way I can.Human leaf is not an easy thing to be send to
15  death.Every one in the world should do his best to save someone from death.

**Comments:** The argument is not clear, and transitions are poor. There are serious syntactic errors (Lines 4–5, 6) and spelling errors (Line 2, *dwon, opoin*, Line 3, *dision*) that impede communication (make it difficult to understand). Language problems cause confusion in spots (sentences in Lines 4–5, and Line 6), so that the meaning is unclear.

## Essay 15

*Score: 57*

Theme is undeveloped and unclear. Short, fairly incomprehensible, some recognizable phrases. General meaning can be gotten with rereading.

**Topic:** A good friend of yours asks for advice about whether to go to work and make money or whether to continue school. What advice would you give him/her?

> I'm glad to write you. I've knew that you are going to U.S. to continue your education. But I don't know what you are ready for it. If fact I know, you have good conditions for our study. Because that you have good basic in English Language and you study very hard I know. Howeaver, you have to take a Michigan Test or TOEFL TEST, then you can find a College or University which you interest in. you must hand in your application form and good scores of Michigan Test or TOEFL. Besides, you have to through much red type in other way.

**Comments:** Very short and undeveloped. Limited syntax and vocabulary. Some basic information conveyed. Fairly good accuracy for a "57" essay.

## Essay 16

*Score: 53*

Short and incomprehensible; single words may be recognizable.

**Topic:** Part-time instead of full-time job.

> If I gose to U.S.A. I'll like to having a part-time job. becuose I sbjact will sdudy to play piano with go to U.S.A. I'll to sdudy it for need morn time. but not a job. my life could have defficalty.

**Comments:** Extremely short and undeveloped. The topic is never really addressed. The meaning is nearly incomprehensible, and idea(s) are unclear. General syntax, grammar, and vocabulary limitations and errors make it difficult to understand.

# Part 2: Listening

## ■ INTRODUCTION

The listening test is designed to show how well you understand spoken English, as used by native speakers of English. The test itself is played on an audio CD. You will be given a test booklet, separate answer sheet, and note sheet. The test booklet contains printed instructions and answer choices for the listening test. You should mark all your answers on the separate answer sheet. You will hear the instructions on the audio as you read them in the test booklet. You will also hear several examples. The examiner will pause the recording after the instructions and examples have been played to see if you have any questions about how to do the test and to see if sound adjustments need to be made. Once the test begins, however, none of the actual test problems will be repeated. The entire test will contain about 50 problems and will take about 30 minutes.

If you have a hearing problem, you should tell the examiner *before* the date of the test, so that special seating arrangements or a special administration can be arranged. You should be prepared to bring to the test a written document from a medical doctor confirming your hearing problem.

With beginning-level students, ESL teachers modify (change) their speech in class. They often speak more slowly and enunciate (pronounce) more carefully in class than they do when they are talking to other native speakers of English. If you have never heard native speakers of English talking to each other, this test may surprise you. It seems to nonnative speakers of any language that the native speakers speak very quickly. It may also seem that words "run together," that is, they are spoken in phrases rather than a single word at a time, with deliberate pauses between words. For example, in conversational English, many contractions occur. A short question like *How would you like to go for a walk?* may sound like *How'dja liketa gofra walk?*

Two good ways to become accustomed to native English speakers is to speak with them, if possible, and to listen to radio and television broadcasts. Several publishing companies in the United States sell teaching materials that include audio components for listening comprehension practice.

The listening test section of the MELAB is entirely multiple choice. It contains:

1. **Short questions.** You should choose the appropriate response (a reasonable answer to the question).

2. **Short dialogues (conversations between two people).** You should choose the appropriate paraphrase or summary. This is a statement that means about the same thing as what the speaker(s) said.

3. **A longer monologue (one person giving a short lecture) and radio reports (a reporter interviewing people).** During the lecture and reports, you may take notes on your answer sheet. Following the lecture and reports, you will be asked content questions about them, and you may refer to your notes to answer the questions.

After each problem or question in the test, you will be allowed 12 seconds to read the answer choices and choose your answer. More time will be allowed for problems with longer written answers or for problems that require you to refer to your notes.

During this test, it is important to concentrate and listen carefully to what you hear. During the short question and dialogue parts, look at the answer choices as you listen to the question or dialogue. Then quickly choose an answer, and mark it on your answer sheet. If you miss a question or don't understand it, quickly guess at the answer, and mark your choice. Then you will be ready for the next question. During the lecture and radio reports, do not look at the answer choices, but listen carefully and write important points or details on the space provided on the separate note sheet. After the lecture or conversation, you will hear questions. Choose the best answer from the choices printed in the test booklet. You may refer to your notes if necessary. Mark your answer choices on the separate answer sheet. Remember, none of the problems in the test will be repeated.

## Examples of Listening Test Problems

Here is an example of the short question type of problem.
*You will hear:*

"Example I: When's she going on vacation?"

*You will read in your test booklet:*

Ex. I a. Last week.
     b. To England.
     c. Tomorrow.

The correct answer is *c. tomorrow* because that is the best response to the question. The speaker asked *when,* so a time expression is needed in the answer. Also, the present continuous tense (as *she is going*) is often used to express future tense, so you know she has not gone on her vacation yet.

Here is an example of the short dialogue type of problem. You should choose the statement that means about the same thing as what you hear.

*You will hear:*

"Example II:"
(Male voice): "That movie was pretty bad."
(Female voice): "It sure was!"

*You will read in your test booklet:*

Ex. II a. She disagrees that it was good.
  b. She agrees that it wasn't good.
  c. She agrees that it was beautiful.

The correct answer is *b. She agrees that it wasn't good.* His statement means the movie was bad, not good. Here *bad* is modified by *pretty*. *Pretty* is used for emphasis, like *very*; here, *pretty* doesn't mean nice looking.

As you listen to the short conversations (dialogues), ask yourself what the relationship between the two speakers is. This might not give you any direct answers to the question that follows, but it may help you to understand the conversation and the setting. Do the speakers know each other? Are they old friends? Are they strangers to each other? Where do you think they are talking: on the street? in a car? in an office or store? What information do they give each other? Do they give directions to locate something or instructions on how to do something? Do they express opinions about other people or circumstances? Do they agree or disagree? Do they sometimes misunderstand each other? Are they angry with each other? Are they being rude or polite? As a listener, you understand better if you have a good idea of what the theme or main idea of the conversation is and what the relationship of the speakers is.

In the actual test, you will not be given an example of the lecture or radio report problems. Here are some suggestions about what to listen for. As you listen, try to decide the main idea. This will usually be emphasized by repetition. In the lecture, the speaker might say, *This is a key issue* or *This is an important point*. Next, decide what the lecturer's supporting arguments are. These might be examples used to illustrate the main idea. The lecturer might say, *for instance, for example*, or, *to illustrate this point*. The lecturer might have an opinion that he or she contrasts with someone else's opinion. Listen for transition words and phrases, such as *first, next, let's turn to, let's move on to, to summarize*, and *finally*. *But* is often used to signal the transition from one idea to another. These are called organization markers.

The reporter conducting the interview in the radio reports will introduce the main theme of the report, and will then introduce the expert, who will explain his or her research. The radio reports may not have the same types of transition markers as the lecture did. Instead, the reporter may ask a question about the expert's findings and, at the end, may summarize the report. When listening to the radio reports, do not worry about the speakers' names, exact numbers, or other unimportant details. Instead, listen for the purpose of the research, how it was conducted, who the participants in the study were, what the findings were, and what the implications of the findings are.

One useful source of different kinds of speech is the ELI-UM Michigan Corpus of Academic Spoken English (MICASE). Sound files are available online, and there are instructional materials for ESL self-study. The website is: **www.lsa.umich.edu/eli/micase/.**

## Practice Listening Tests

Two practice tests follow. Before you begin the practice tests, review the examples just given. An answer key and a script for the practice tests are on pp. 83–114, but do not look at them yet.

First, take the practice test. An answer sheet for the listening and GCVR practice tests is in Appendix E on page 145. For the actual MELAB, you will be given a note page to use for the lecture and radio reports. For these practice tests, you should supply your own note paper. Play the audio straight through, without stopping or repeating any of the questions. Then score your test using the key. If you wish, you may take the test several times without stopping, but be sure you use a new answer sheet each time.

Next, you should score your test using the key. Finally, review the practice test by playing the audio as you read the script. Compare your answers with those in the key. At this time, you may stop the recording and repeat questions if you wish. The pauses on the audio replicate the length of time students have to answer each question on the test.

Do *not* look at the key or script until you have taken the entire test at least once and have marked your answers on the answer sheet. If you look at the key or script too soon, you cannot make an accurate assessment of your listening ability, and your score will not be correct or interpretable.

## Part 2, Practice Test 1

Before you begin this practice test, review the examples. Do *not* look at the key or script until you have finished the entire test.

This is a test of how well you understand spoken English. There are several kinds of problems. In the first kind of problem, you will hear a question, and you must choose, from the three answer choices printed in your test booklet, a reasonable answer to the question. For example, listen to the question and choose one of the answers below.

Example I:  Listen to the question.

   a. last week
   b. tomorrow
   c. to England

The correct answer is *b. tomorrow* because the speaker asked, *When's she going on vacation?*

In the second kind of problem, you will hear a very short conversation. For this kind of problem, choose the answer that means about the same thing as what you heard. For example, listen to the conversation.

> Example II: Listen to the conversation.
>
> > a. She agrees that it was beautiful.
> > b. She disagrees that it wasn't good.
> > c. She agrees that it wasn't good.

The correct answer is *c. She agrees that it wasn't good* because the speakers said, *That movie was pretty bad* and *It sure was!*

Finally, you will hear one short talk, or lecture, and two short radio reports on unrelated topics. You will be able to take notes as you listen. You may write your notes on the separate note page. After you hear each segment, you will be asked some questions about it. Mark all your answers on the separate answer sheet. Do NOT write in your test booklet. Please be very quiet and listen carefully. No problem can be repeated. Do you have any questions?

Now we will begin Practice Test 1. Turn the page to Problem Number 1.

For Problems 1 through 15, you will hear a short question. Choose a reasonable answer to the question.

1. a. In Sue's car.
   b. Sue's parents are.
   c. Before noon.

2. a. See a movie.
   b. I'd like to.
   c. Steak and potatoes.

3. a. Yes, I've been there twice.
   b. No, it's about twice as expensive.
   c. No, it takes twice as long.

4. a. Not in the office.
   b. At two o'clock.
   c. My last test.

5. a. Yes, I do.
   b. No, she doesn't.
   c. Yes, she will.

6. a. Yes, you can use them.
   b. No, you don't.
   c. Because yours aren't any better.

7. a. Make a special appointment with me.
   b. My office is in Room 203.
   c. My office hours are from 9 to 11.

8. a. If you want to.
   b. No, I'm not.
   c. Yes, I'm finished.

9. a. Late last night.
   b. Sounds like fun.
   c. They'll go with you.

10. a. The river flooded.
    b. When it rained last night.
    c. It might have.

11. a. Near Central Park.
    b. The subway.
    c. Straight down 5th Avenue.

12. a. He wasn't here.
    b. In order to get them.
    c. For the secretary.

13. a. I'll see if it works.
    b. Sure, I can help.
    c. OK, give me one.

14. a. just some footprints
    b. No, the thief got away.
    c. It was over when they got there.

15. a. OK, I'll borrow yours.
    b. Sorry, I missed it too.
    c. It was the last one.

For Problems 16 through 35, you will hear short conversations. Choose the statement that means about the same thing as what you hear.

16. a. He doesn't need to see the doctor.
    b. He missed his appointment.
    c. He'll see the doctor the next day.

17. a. Jane didn't stay late.
    b. Jane came later.
    c. Jane didn't go.

18. a. They won't go.
    b. They'll go sooner.
    c. They'll go somewhere else.

19. a. He missed the start.
    b. He missed the whole match.
    c. He'll wait to see it later.

20. a. It's too late for him to go.
    b. He's already gone.
    c. He shouldn't delay any longer.

21. a. He can't find the right office.
    b. He should return to her office at 1:00.
    c. He can register after 1:00.

22. a. She needs to take other classes first.
    b. She needs to take Professor Morton's class first.
    c. She already took Professor Morton's class.

23. a. He's having trouble too.
    b. He came sooner than she did.
    c. He was better prepared.

24. a. He suggests a different order.
    b. He thinks she works too hard.
    c. He thinks she doesn't work hard enough.

25. a. They don't have to turn one in.
    b. It must be turned in on time.
    c. It can be turned in later.

26. a. He'll talk to her now.
    b. He'll talk to her later.
    c. He won't talk to her.

27. a. He wasn't badly injured.
    b. Someone was badly injured.
    c. No one was badly injured.

28. a. She wants him to get out of the car.
    b. He thinks she drives too fast.
    c. He'll give her a ticket.

29. a. They can't get back in the house.
    b. They'll go back to get the keys.
    c. She has extra keys.

30. a. He can't do it either.
    b. He will do it for her.
    c. She can use his calculator.

31. a. She'll buy a new one.
    b. She'll have it repaired.
    c. He'll fix it for her.

32. a. He thinks Bob won't quit.
    b. He thinks Bob will quit.
    c. He thinks Bob has a new job.

33. a. He'll replace her for a while.
    b. He'll take it there for her.
    c. He can fix the broken equipment.

34. a. He doesn't need to take anything.
    b. He should take some identification.
    c. She can register him now.

35. a. They think the discussion was useful.
    b. They'll leave together.
    c. They're having an argument.

In the last part of the test, you will hear a short talk, or lecture, and two short radio reports on unrelated topics. As you listen, you may take notes on the separate note page. Do not write in this test booklet. When each segment is finished, you will be asked some questions about it. You may use your notes to answer the questions.

Now you will hear a short talk by an environmentalist.

36. a. polluted water
    b. traffic jams, more houses and boats
    c. fewer shellfish

37. a. Water becomes polluted.
    b. Clams become polluted and can't be eaten.
    c. The number of marine fauna species is reduced.

38. a. high bacteria counts
    b. land development
    c. a stressed environment

39. a. It has died off.
    b. It can't be used as a seed clam.
    c. It is so polluted it can't be eaten.

40. a. Beaches are closed to swimmers.
    b. Clams and fish have died off.
    c. The beachfront is crowded with houses and boats.

Now you will hear the first short radio report.

41. a. computer programmers' claims
    b. methods of improving memory
    c. effects of aging on memory

42. a. Subjects were tested on material they had studied.
    b. Subjects practiced using a variety of strategies.
    c. Subjects analyzed computer games.

43. a. using effective strategies
    b. using effective computer games
    c. using a variety of programs and strategies

44. a. They didn't improve even with more training.
    b. They improved the least.
    c. They improved the most.

45. a. They concentrated on the best computer games.
    b. They concentrated on taking the test.
    c. They concentrated on memorizing the material.

Now you will hear the second short radio report.

46. a. as a study of the body's immune system
    b. as a study applying man-made to biological materials
    c. as a study of bacteria-resistant antibiotics

47. a. Bacteria don't become resistant to AMPs.
    b. AMPs are not broken down by enzymes.
    c. AMPs are not toxic, even in large doses.

48. a. man-made cookware
    b. bacteria resistant to antibiotics
    c. interest in exploiting natural antibiotics

49. a. They become less resistant to bacteria.
    b. They become sticky.
    c. They destroy red blood cells.

50. a. They resist more kinds of bacteria.
    b. They are more concentrated in the body.
    c. They last longer in the body.

End of Practice Test 1

## Part 2, Practice Test 2

Before you begin this practice test, review the examples. Do *not* look at the key or script until you have finished the entire test.

This is a test of how well you understand spoken English. There are several kinds of problems. In the first kind of problem, you will hear a question, and you must choose, from the three answer choices printed in your test booklet, a reasonable answer to the question. For example, listen to the question and choose one of the answers below.

> Example I: Listen to the question.
>
>   a. last week
>   b. tomorrow
>   c. to England

The correct answer is *b. tomorrow* because the speaker asked *When's she going on vacation?*

In the second kind of problem, you will hear a very short conversation. For this kind of problem choose the answer that means about the same thing as what you heard. For example, listen to the conversation.

> Example II: Listen to the conversation.
>
>   a. She agrees that it was beautiful.
>   b. She disagrees that it wasn't good.
>   c. She agrees that it wasn't good.

The correct answer is *c. She agrees that it wasn't good* because the speakers said, *That movie was pretty bad* and *It sure was!*

Finally, you will hear one short talk, or lecture, and two short radio reports on unrelated topics. You will be able to take notes as you listen. You may write your notes on the separate note page. After you hear each segment, you will be asked some questions about it.

Mark all your answers on the separate answer sheet. Do NOT write in your test booklet. Please be very quiet and listen carefully. No problem can be repeated. Do you have any questions?

Now we will begin Practice Test 2. Turn the page to Problem Number 1.

For Problems 1 through 15, you will hear a short question.  Choose a reasonable answer to the question.

1.  a.  No, I don't think you can.
    b.  If you want to.
    c.  At the end of the hall.

2.  a.  Maybe he came to the party.
    b.  If he's not busy.
    c.  Yes, he gave them to me.

3.  a.  Sure, I'll do it.
    b.  After I go to the cleaners.
    c.  On my way home.

4.  a.  It's hard to say.
    b.  Yes, she can improve it.
    c.  No, I can't prove it.

5.  a.  I take the bus.
    b.  My brother told me how.
    c.  I enjoy it.

6.  a.  Sorry, I'm not going to class.
    b.  Sorry, I don't mind.
    c.  Yes, please give it to her.

7.  a.  Yes, Mary has.
    b.  No, I can't.
    c.  Yes, it was late.

8.  a.  Sure, no problem.
    b.  At my office.
    c.  On Friday.

9.  a.  It's quite important.
    b.  50 words per minute.
    c.  Open it quickly.

10. a.  Do the writing first.
    b.  Both of them will.
    c.  OK, I'll go there first.

11. a.  Sure, I'll come.
    b.  It's nearly finished.
    c.  When you're ready.

12. a.  I have two reasons.
    b.  That's my opinion.
    c.  They caused it.

13. a.  They can if they want to.
    b.  They haven't stopped yet.
    c.  Let them settle it by themselves.

14. a.  It's in the records.
    b.  Sure, it's done all the time.
    c.  If you put them there.

15. a.  They found two possibilities.
    b.  They were alone.
    c.  That's the cause.

For Problems 16 through 35, you will hear short conversations. Choose the statement that means about the same thing as what you hear.

16. a. He can't find them either.
    b. He'll give them to her.
    c. He thinks he knows where they are.

17. a. There was lack of interest.
    b. The class was at a different place.
    c. The class will be later.

18. a. She'll get the tickets.
    b. He'll ask a friend for tickets.
    c. He'll give the tickets to his friend.

19. a. They'll start the match today.
    b. They finished the match yesterday.
    c. They couldn't finish the match yesterday.

20. a. He liked the old one better.
    b. It's a lot of work.
    c. It's a better job.

21. a. He thinks the exams are over.
    b. He thinks Mary studies too much.
    c. He thinks Mary isn't prepared.

22. a. She prefers the lectures.
    b. She prefers the lab work.
    c. She prefers the readings.

23. a. He did better than she did.
    b. She thinks it had new information.
    c. She couldn't remember anything.

24. a. She didn't buy all the books.
    b. He bought some cheaper books.
    c. He didn't buy some of the texts.

25. a. He wants her opinion of it.
    b. He wants her to finish it.
    c. He thinks it's taking too long.

26. a. He didn't follow her directions.
    b. He wants her to drive.
    c. He followed her directions.

27. a. The house was burned down.
    b. The garage was burned down.
    c. The house and garage were burned down.

28. a. She wants to drive.
    b. She wants him to drive.
    c. He wants her to be quiet.

29. a. They think Mr. Jones isn't smart.
    b. They think Mr. Jones is too proud.
    c. They think Mr. Jones is not imaginative.

30. a. It will be started soon.
    b. It cost more than expected.
    c. It will be started later.

31. a. Lyons will probably be a candidate.
    b. Lyons will have their support.
    c. Lyons is the most popular candidate.

32. a. Betty is gone.
    b. Betty is afraid to leave.
    c. Betty is going to leave.

33. a. He's moving now.
    b. He can't help her now.
    c. He'll help for an hour.

34. a. They don't know when Arnold will arrive.
    b. They know Arnold's arrival time.
    c. They got incorrect information.

35. a. He can't do it in a week.
    b. He did it a week ago.
    c. He'll probably need a week.

In the last part of the test, you will hear a short talk, or lecture, and two short radio reports, on unrelated topics. As you listen, you may take notes on the separate note page. Do not write in this test booklet. When each segment is finished, you will be asked some questions about it. You may use your notes to answer the questions.

Now you will hear a short talk about an interesting art form.

36. a. radiographs of flowers
    b. a visit to a five and dime store
    c. a bunch of daffodils

37. a. black and white photography
    b. X-ray photography
    c. a purely dental technique

38. a. record reflected transmitted light
    b. yield black and white images
    c. penetrate X-rays

39. a. X-rays don't require light.
    b. X-rays reflect transmitted light.
    c. X-rays penetrate the subject.

40. a. They are transparent.
    b. They reflect light.
    c. They are black and white.

Now you will hear the first short radio report.

41. a. what they thought of their culture
    b. what made them happy
    c. what experiences they had growing up

42. a. that some Japanese are more like Americans than like Japanese
    b. that there is variation in Japanese culture
    c. that Japan is different from other East Asian cultures

43. a. developing new territory
    b. successful group efforts
    c. individual achievement

44. a. being isolated from the main culture
    b. settling undeveloped territory
    c. coming from peasant and military background

45. a. an outlook that values independence
    b. an outlook that values cooperation
    c. an outlook that values the dominant culture

Now you will hear the second short radio report.

46. a. what motivates people to exercise
    b. the effects of a sedentary life style
    c. the effects of different levels of exercise

47. a. The duration of the exercise did not matter.
    b. Moderate exercisers did better than intense exercisers.
    c. Triglyceride levels stayed low.

48. a. after each workout in the exercise program
    b. during intense and then during moderate exercise
    c. at the start, during, and after the program ended

49. a. ran or walked fast on a track
    b. alternated walking fast and slow
    c. rode stationary bicycles

50. a. Longer and more intense exercise is the best kind.
    b. Moderate exercise is the best kind.
    c. It is dangerous to stop exercising too soon.

End of Practice Test 2

# Part 3: Grammar, Cloze, Vocabulary, Reading (GCVR)

This part of the MELAB battery has four different kinds of problems: grammar, cloze reading, vocabulary, and reading comprehension. If you take a 100-item test, the time limit is 75 minutes (1 hour and 15 minutes); if the test is longer, like 130 or 144 items, the time limit will be extended accordingly. When you take this part of the test, it is important to answer the problems as quickly as you can. Do not spend a great deal of time on individual grammar or vocabulary problems; remember that the reading will take longer because you must read a paragraph in addition to answering questions about it. Look for the right answer, or one that seems correct, rather than looking at all the answers and trying to eliminate the wrong ones. Often, two answers will seem correct while the other two are clearly wrong. Choose the most likely. In the practice test, you may mark the ones you are uncertain about in your test book or on your answer sheet, but the actual MELAB is scored by an optical scanner, so you should not make any stray marks on the answer sheet. If you do, an item may be marked as incorrect. If you have time at the end of the test, you can go back and spend more time on the problems you were unsure of. If you do not know the answer, guess. You are not penalized for guessing: your final score is based on the total number of correct answers.

For the grammar problems, you should review word order in statements, questions and embedded phrases, noun compounds, prepositions, connectors, adverbs and adjectives, verb tenses, subject-verb agreement, use of active and passive voice, modals, infinitives, and gerunds. Though the grammar problems are in a conversational format, they include some formal as well as informal usage. About half the grammar problems will concern verbs.

Here is an example of a grammar problem. You should choose the word or phrase that correctly completes the conversation.

"How did you know that Helen was here?"
"She _____ by some of her friends."
   a. seen
   b. is seeing
   c. has seen
   d. was seen

The correct answer is *d. was seen*. This is the passive past tense form of the verb *to see*. Passive voice must be used because the friends are the ones who saw Helen, who is the subject of the sentence, and past tense should be used because the action (Helen was seen) took place in the past.

In the cloze reading section, you will read a paragraph from which 20 words have been deleted (taken out). You should choose, from the choices given, the one word that fits each blank both in grammar and in meaning. Skim quickly through the cloze passage to get the main idea before you try to select the correct words for the blanks. As you skim the cloze passage, think of what word form fits each blank (noun, adjective, verb, connector, etc.), and think of a meaning that might fit before you look at the answer choices. Be sure to read the entire sentence that the missing word appears in; an incorrect choice may seem to fit in a phrase but will not fit in the context of the whole sentence. You might get some clues to a missing word in the sentence that comes before or after it. The missing word will usually not be a difficult or unusual word; if it is unusual, you can probably guess it from the context of the cloze passage.

Here is an example of a short cloze passage.

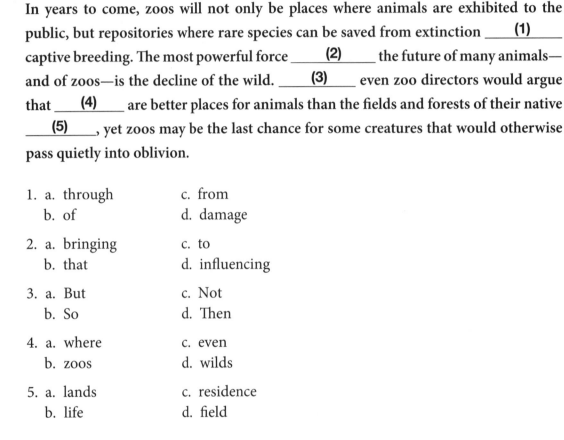

**In years to come, zoos will not only be places where animals are exhibited to the public, but repositories where rare species can be saved from extinction ____(1)____ captive breeding. The most powerful force ____(2)____ the future of many animals—and of zoos—is the decline of the wild. ____(3)____ even zoo directors would argue that ____(4)____ are better places for animals than the fields and forests of their native ____(5)____, yet zoos may be the last chance for some creatures that would otherwise pass quietly into oblivion.**

1. a. through          c. from
   b. of               d. damage

2. a. bringing         c. to
   b. that             d. influencing

3. a. But              c. Not
   b. So               d. Then

4. a. where            c. even
   b. zoos             d. wilds

5. a. lands            c. residence
   b. life             d. field

The correct answers are: *1a, 2d, 3c, 4b, 5a*. For 1, a preposition that means "by means of" is needed as a sentence-level connector. For 2, a verb that means "affecting" is needed. For 3, you need to read ahead in the sentence to understand that zoo officials do *not* think zoos are better than the animals' natural homes. For 4, *zoos* contrasts with *fields and forests*. For 5, a plural noun meaning "a specific place" is needed. *Residence* is inappropriate for animals.

The words tested in vocabulary problems occur 5–12 times per million; that is, for every million words used, these words will appear 5 to 12 times. Idiomatic expressions will also be tested. The test writers use the following references as guides.

John B. Carroll et al., *The American Heritage Word Frequency Book.* New York: American Heritage Publishing, 1971.

Henry Kučera and W. Nelson Francis, *Frequency Analysis of English Usage, Lexicon, and Grammar.* Boston: Houghton Mifflin, 1982. (This is the "Brown University Corpus.")

Edward L. Thorndike and Irving Lorge, *The Teacher's Word Book of 30,000 Words.* New York: Teachers College Columbia University, 1944, 2d ed. 1952.

Averil Coxhead. Academic Word List (AWL) in "A new academic word list," *TESOL Quarterly,* 34 (2): 213–238. Reprinted in W. Teubert and R. Krishnamurthy (Eds.), *Corpus Linguistics: Critical Concepts in Linguistics,* pp. 123–49. Oxford: Routledge, 2007.

Averil Coxhead. University Word List (UWL) in Xue Guoyi and I.S.P. Nation, "A University Word List," *Language Learning and Communication* 3, no. 2 (1984): 215–29.

Dictionaries, such as *Longman Advanced American Dictionary, Cambridge Dictionaries,* Heinle's *Newbury House Dictionary of American English.*

Michigan Corpus of Academic Spoken English (MICASE). www.lsa.umich.edu/eli/micase/.

Some forms of the GCVR have two kinds of vocabulary problems. In one kind, you will see a sentence with an underlined word or phrase. From the answer choices given below the sentence, you should choose the word or phrase that means about the same thing as the underlined word or phrase in the sentence, and which could be used in the sentence without changing its meaning. The underlined word or phrase will often be more specific, and it will occur less frequently (e.g, 5–12 times per million words) in English than the answer choices. The answer choices will be high frequency words that occur 50 or more times per million. You will probably know these common words. Approximately 75–80 percent of the vocabulary words are of Greco-Latin origin and about 10 percent are idiomatic expressions.

Here is an example of the first kind of vocabulary problem.

It's too windy to go for a stroll.
   a. swim
   b. sail
   c. drive
   d. walk

The correct answer is *d.* A *stroll* is a leisurely walk.

In the other kind of vocabulary problem, you will read a sentence with a word or phrase missing and a list of four words or phrases. You are to choose the word or phrase that best fits into the sentence in a meaningful way. Idiomatic expressions will also appear.

Here is an example of the sentence completion type of vocabulary problem:

The first things we study in school are very _____.
   a.  sturdy
   b.  shifty
   c.  elementary
   d.  trusty

The correct answer choice is *c. elementary. Very* in the sentence leads you to expect an adjective, and *first things* are elementary, or basic things.

In the reading comprehension section of Part 3, there are several reading passages, each followed by three to six questions, depending on the length of the passage. Most reading passages are about 260 words long and have five questions. The passages on each form of the test will cover different topics, or areas of study. Some will be in the social sciences, some natural sciences, humanities, history, medicine, etc. It is the type of reading that a university student might find in a newspaper, book, or magazine article. The reading levels, as measured by standard U.S. reading level tests, range from 11th grade (in high school) to first-year college. The questions following each passage will ask about the main idea, supporting details or facts, cause and effect relationships, the author's opinion, and drawing inferences. All the information you need to answer the questions will be in the passage; you will not need prior knowledge of the subject matter.

Several techniques can be helpful with this type of test, and you should practice them to find the method that works best for you. One method is to read the questions first, then read the passage, thinking of the questions, and then answer them. A second method is to skim through the passage for the main idea, then read the questions and reread the passage more carefully before answering the questions. A third method is to read the passage carefully, then answer the questions, looking back to the passage if necessary for details.

Here is an example of a short reading passage.

**The influenza virus is a single molecule built from many millions of single atoms. Viruses are sometimes called "living molecules." While bacteria can be considered as a type of plant, secreting poisonous substances into the body of the organism they attack, viruses are living organisms themselves. We may consider them as regular chemical molecules, since they have a strictly defined atomic structure, but on the other hand we must also consider them as being alive, since they are able to multiply in unlimited quantities.**

1. According to the passage, bacteria are . . .
   a. poisons.
   b. larger than viruses.
   c. very small.
   d. plants.

2. The writer says that viruses are alive because they . . .
   a. have a complex atomic structure.
   b. move.
   c. multiply.
   d. need warmth and light.

3. The atomic structure of viruses . . .
   a. is variable.
   b. is strictly defined.
   c. cannot be analyzed chemically.
   d. is more complex than that of bacteria.

The correct answers are *1d, 2c, 3b.* For 1, the passage stated that *bacteria can be considered as a type of plant.* For 2, you are asked *why* they are considered living. This is explained in the passage by the phrase, *since they are able to multiply.* For 3, the passage states that viruses *have a strictly defined atomic structure.*

## Practice Tests

Two practice tests for Part 3 follow. A sample answer sheet is in Appendix E. Each practice test has 30 grammar, 20 cloze, 30 vocabulary, and 20 reading problems, making a total of 100 problems (Practice Test 1 has both types of vocabulary problems. Practice Test 2 has only one kind of vocabulary problem.). The time limit for completing these 100 problems is 75 minutes (1 hour and 15 minutes). Time yourself carefully before you start, and stop when 75 minutes have passed. Following the practice tests are an answer key and commentary (pp. 115–26). Do not look at either until you have finished the test. Then, score your test, and read the commentary for the problems you missed or were uncertain about.

## ■ PART 3: GRAMMAR, CLOZE, VOCABULARY, READING—PRACTICE TEST 1

**INSTRUCTIONS:** Do not begin this test until the examiner has read these instructions with you.

1.  Fill in the correct form on your answer sheet.

2.  This test contains 100 problems. There are four kinds: grammar, cloze, vocabulary, and reading comprehension. Examples of each kind of problem are given below.

3.  Each problem in the test has **only one** correct answer. Use a number 2 (soft) pencil to mark answers on the answer sheet. Make only one mark on your answer sheet for each problem. If you want to change an answer, completely erase the old mark.

4.  **Do not make any marks in this test booklet.** Write only on your answer sheet.

5.  The examiner will not explain any test problem; only the examples may be explained if you do not understand the problems.

6.  You will have 75 minutes to finish the entire test. Try to answer all the problems. Each problem counts the same. Do not spend too much time on any one problem or you will not have time to finish the test. Unanswered problems will be counted wrong. You may answer the problems in any order you wish.

7.  Here are examples of each kind of problem. In each example, the correct answer has been marked with an asterisk (*). For the actual problems, fill in the circle corresponding to the answer you choose. **Do not write in this test booklet.**

**GRAMMAR:** Choose the word or phrase that correctly completes the conversation.

    I.  "What is that thing?"
       "That _____ a spider."
         a. to call
         b. for calling
         c. be called
      *d. is called

**CLOZE:** Read the passage, then select the word that best fills the blank in both grammar and meaning.

Long ago, roads were only trails for people and animals to walk on, but today roads must be made for cars, trucks, and buses. The most modern _____ is often called a superhighway.

    II.  a. way         *b. road         c. travel         d. superhighway

**VOCABULARY:** There are two different kinds of vocabulary problems. In one kind, you should choose the word or phrase that means the same thing as the underlined word or phrase (see Ex. III). In the other kind, you should choose the word or phrase that most appropriately completes the sentence (see Ex. IV).

III. It's too windy to go for a <u>stroll</u>.
   a. swim
   b. sail
   c. drive
   *d. walk

IV. Because of the storm and rough waves, it would be foolish to go out sailing today in a small _____.
   a. automobile
   b. house
   *c. boat
   d. beast

**READING:** Read the passage, then answer the questions following it according to the information given in the passage.

**While I was getting ready to go to town one morning last week, my wife handed me a little piece of red cloth and asked if I would have time during the day to buy her two yards of cloth like that.**

V. The person telling the story is . . .
   a. a married lady.
   b. an unmarried lady.
   *c. a married man.
   d. an unmarried man.

8. Remember, you have 75 minutes (one hour and 15 minutes) to finish the entire test. Do not write in the test booklet. Mark only on the answer sheet. You may begin now.

## Part 3, Practice Test 1

For Problems 1 through 30, choose the word or phrase that correctly completes the sentence.

1. "In America, are most scientists well paid?"
   "Yes, the _____ are paid very well."
   a. majority of scientists
   b. majority of scientist
   c. scientists of majority
   d. scientists majority

2. "What is your job at the factory?"
   "My job is _____ all the doors at the end of the day."
   a. locking
   b. to be locking
   c. locks
   d. locked

3. "I paid $30 for a taxi from the airport last night."
   "You _____ me for a ride."
   a. would have asked
   b. could asked
   c. could ask
   d. could have asked

4. "Let's take the elevator to the 25th floor."
   "Never! Elevators are something _____."
   a. which I'm afraid
   b. I'm afraid of
   c. which I'm afraid of it
   d. which I'm afraid of them

5. "Why did John quit school?"
   "He told me it was because of _____."
   a. his failure constantly
   b. his constantly failure
   c. he failed constantly
   d. his constant failure

6. "We need more art classes."
   "I don't think so. The students _____ in art."
   a. are not interesting
   b. have not interested
   c. are not interested
   d. have not interest

7. "I can't do all this work!"
   "_____ I helped you with it?"
   a. What if
   b. That if
   c. As if
   d. However

8. "Groceries are certainly expensive."
   "Yes, each time I go shopping, I seem _____ more."
   a. spending
   b. be spending
   c. to spending
   d. to be spending

9. "The children want to play."
   "Yes, but _____ do is their homework."
   a. what should they
   b. what they should
   c. they should
   d. that should they

10. "Can you give me a receipt?"
    "Yes, that can be _____."
    a. easy done
    b. easy doing
    c. easily done
    d. easy to be done

11. "Did John finish his homework?"
    "Yes; although he was tired, _____ it all."
    a. but he did
    b. despite he did
    c. he did
    d. that he did

12. "Do you always believe Donald?"
    "Yes, I have complete trust _____ whatever he says."
    a. on
    b. to
    c. in
    d. at

13. "Why is the front door open?"
    "Oh, I'm sorry. I _____ forgotten to lock it."
    a. should have
    b. must have
    c. ought to have
    d. had to have

14. "Do you like that cake?"
    "Well, it has too much sugar in it, but _____ it's ok."
    a. other than that
    b. another of that
    c. that other
    d. none other than

15. "What did you think when you met Robert's mother?"
    "I was very impressed _____ her friendliness."
    a. on
    b. of
    c. by
    d. at

16. "What do you want Phil for?"
    "I want him _____ the house while I'm away."
    a. guards
    b. guarded
    c. the guard of
    d. guarding

17. "Why don't you paint your room blue?"
    "Oh, I never thought _____ that."
    a. to be done
    b. of doing
    c. to have done
    d. to do

18. "Can you help me choose my wife a gift?"
    "Certainly; first tell me _____ expensive a gift you would like to buy."
    a. how
    b. how much
    c. as
    d. as much as

19. "I took your books back to the library."
    "Oh, no! I wish you _____ that."
    a. didn't do
    b. didn't have done
    c. haven't done
    d. hadn't done

20. "What's so interesting about the San Marcos River?"
    "It has plant life which you can't _____ any other place."
    a. find
    b. find it
    c. find them
    d. be found

21. "Do you have any plans for the weekend?"
    "I hope to _____ my house."
    a. finish to paint
    b. finish paint
    c. finish painting
    d. finishing paint

22. "Have you heard from John lately?"
    "Yes, I've had news of his _____ by a famous company."
    a. hire
    b. been hiring
    c. hired
    d. being hired

23. "Is the coffee all right?"
    "It's not _____ hot enough."
    a. rather
    b. quite
    c. too
    d. fairly

24. "I hate cooked carrots."
    "Would you like _____ raw?"
    a. as
    b. they are
    c. to be
    d. them

25. "What do you dislike about that store?"
    "Other _____ their high prices, nothing."
    a. than
    b. from
    c. except
    d. besides

26. "Dr. Jones wants to see you in his office immediately."
    "Why _____ see him?"
    a. must I
    b. I must
    c. have I to
    d. I have to

27. "Let's ask Hugh if we can use his car."
    "Willy's car is easier to _____."
    a. starts
    b. start
    c. be started
    d. be starting

28. "Isn't little Millicent charming!"
    "Yes, I have never seen _____ child."
    a. a so lovely
    b. such lovely a
    c. so lovely a
    d. a such lovely

29. "What do you think of this apartment?"
    "Oh, it's very expensive; _____ it's much larger than what I really want."
    a. even so
    b. moreover
    c. in spite of
    d. although

30. "Do you come here often?"
    "No. In fact, _____."
    a. hardly ever
    b. ever hardly
    c. never hardly
    d. hardly never

For Problems 31 through 50, choose the word that best fits each blank both in grammar and in meaning.

An American climatologist has found evidence that five major shifts in the climate of the northern hemisphere over the last 12,000 years may have led to profound cultural changes. His conclusions are based on a __(31)__ of the records from some 470 __(32)__ and the geological evidence for when __(33)__ changes occurred. Scientists have long known __(34)__ every few hundred years, earth's prevailing __(35)__ has undergone dramatic changes within a __(36)__ of only a few years. All __(37)__ become generally cooler or warmer; annual __(38)__ rises or falls significantly. Sea level __(39)__ or falls. The last such change __(40)__ place about 800 years ago. England __(41)__ Europe became cooler and more moist __(42)__ they had been for 300 years, __(43)__ in North America, the climate became __(44)__ and cooler. All over the northern __(45)__ the climates changed. The reason is __(46)__ to have been a massive, global __(47)__ in the wind patterns of the __(48)__ atmosphere. Major climatic conditions are governed __(49)__ such winds which, every few centuries, __(50)__ their direction. Nobody knows for sure why this happens.

31. a. statistic  c. comparison
    b. result  d. data
32. a. evidence  c. scientific
    b. data  d. cultures
33. a. change  c. this
    b. climatic  d. do
34. a. that  c. in
    b. changes  d. it
35. a. climate  c. variation
    b. which  d. change
36. a. pattern  c. period
    b. notice  d. lot
37. a. shifts  c. seasons
    b. changes  d. earth
38. a. weather  c. rainfall
    b. sun  d. crop
39. a. increase  c. ups
    b. high  d. rises
40. a. took  c. in
    b. takes  d. was
41. a. and  c. not
    b. in  d. but
42. a. than  c. how
    b. climate  d. as
43. a. Canada  c. somewhere
    b. while  d. even
44. a. drier  c. humidity
    b. warmer  d. less
45. a. have  c. hemisphere
    b. did  d. all
46. a. that  c. due
    b. going  d. believed
47. a. rotates  c. air
    b. climate  d. shift
48. a. above  c. upper
    b. climate  d. windy
49. a. mostly  c. in
    b. by  d. for
50. a. change  c. turn
    b. especially  d. in

For Problems 51 through 65, choose the word or phrase that means the same thing as the underlined word or phrase.

51. Peter was <u>positive</u> he would see Fred.
    a. certain
    b. afraid
    c. surprised
    d. happy

52. He <u>trailed</u> me.
    a. answered
    b. found
    c. followed
    d. carried

53. He <u>grabbed</u> my book.
    a. talked about
    b. suddenly took
    c. lost
    d. returned

54. The dog <u>trembled</u> when it saw the bone.
    a. shook
    b. begged
    c. barked
    d. jumped

55. The farmers <u>encountered</u> a group of soldiers.
    a. fought
    b. helped
    c. fed
    d. met

56. His remarks about the economy <u>baffled</u> me.
    a. confused
    b. relieved
    c. worried
    d. interested

57. She did not know why she felt so <u>despondent</u>.
    a. hopeless
    b. bored
    c. happy
    d. excited

58. He told me it was <u>a snap</u>.
    a. difficult
    b. good
    c. easy
    d. bad

59. Edward made a <u>feeble</u> reply.
    a. calm
    b. weak
    c. sincere
    d. slow

60. He's not a very <u>credible</u> lecturer.
    a. well-known
    b. religious
    c. ordinary
    d. believable

61. He <u>contemplated</u> becoming a jet pilot.
    a. preferred
    b. suggested
    c. considered
    d. tried

62. She <u>shoved</u> him.
    a. pushed
    b. watched
    c. called
    d. reminded

63. Oscar did the job <u>grudgingly</u>.
    a. immediately
    b. unwillingly
    c. easily
    d. carefully

64. He thinks that method is <u>prevalent</u>.
    a. advanced
    b. common
    c. difficult
    d. old-fashioned

65. He was only <u>speculating</u> about the cost.
    a. worrying
    b. complaining
    c. asking
    d. guessing

For Problems 66 through 80, choose the word or phrase that correctly completes the sentence.

66. Tim doesn't know anything about literature and he is just as _____ of biology.
    a. partial
    b. ignorant
    c. approximate
    d. abbreviated

67. I think that bridge can hold this truck; it looks very _____ to me.
    a. muscular
    b. sturdy
    c. noble
    d. elaborate

68. The city tried to stop crime by hiring more police, but that _____ did not work.
    a. approach
    b. application
    c. management
    d. version

69. John wrote home to say he liked school. But his parents knew he was homesick because they _____.
    a. called him to account
    b. begged the question
    c. marked his words
    d. read between the lines

70. It is very difficult to understand Roger because he _____ whenever he speaks.
    a. muffles
    b. dims
    c. sprinkles
    d. mutters

71. Alex isn't very friendly; he keeps a _____ between himself and other people.
    a. gauge
    b. foundation
    c. frontier
    d. barrier

72. There are many good bakeries in Milltown; in fact, the baking industry is _____.
    a. adhesive
    b. flourishing
    c. incidental
    d. accommodating

73. Don't water the new seeds too much; just _____ them.
    a. sprinkle
    b. trigger
    c. wrinkle
    d. filter

74. Francis didn't have to do anything to get the money; it was _____ gift.
    a. an outright
    b. a predominant
    c. a retentive
    d. a saturated

75. For many years, they have _____ an office in that building.
    a. persisted
    b. remained
    c. maintained
    d. withheld

76. His friendliness and helpfulness are _____ that make everyone like him.
    a. principles
    b. attributes
    c. functions
    d. regimens

77. Lucy delayed the bus because she was
    _____ in her purse for the correct
    change.
    a. baffling
    b. stuffing
    c. lurching
    d. fumbling

78. Arnold couldn't decide and _____
    for several minutes before acting.
    a. hesitated
    b. alternated
    c. suspended
    d. apprehended

79. While the main army attacked from
    the east, a small group of soldiers
    made a _____ in the north.
    a. diffraction
    b. dismissal
    c. diversion
    d. deterrent

80. After his heart attack he had to stop
    playing football, tennis, and other
    _____ sports.
    a. precarious
    b. strenuous
    c. ardent
    d. compressed

For Problems 81 through 100, read the passages, and then answer the questions following them according to the information given in the passage.

Sponges are just barely animals, such a borderline case that until the 19th century they were called zoophytes, the animal-plants. They are among the most primitive forms of multi-cellular animal life; they have no muscles or nerves, no mouth or digestive cavity, nothing in the way of organs. But they have been around a long time and must be doing something right. More than 5,000 species inhabit this planet, living in fresh water and throughout the sea down to depths of more than 25,000 feet.

Often strikingly beautiful, sponges offer the added virtue of usefulness. Even with synthetic sponges widely available, a market for natural sponges persists. They hold more water without dripping, are easier to clean, and last longer, even under heavy use. And now, after centuries in the bathtub, sponges are finding their way into the laboratories of pharmacologists and cell biologists. As do so many marine invertebrates that have limited defenses in the usual sense (they are capable of neither fight nor flight), sponges produce some extremely powerful chemical compounds, toxic and otherwise, that hold great promise as future drugs for the treatment of human disorders, including cancer.

81. According to the passage, why are sponges of interest to pharmacologists and biologists?
    a. because of their digestive system
    b. because of the chemicals they produce
    c. because they are neither plant nor animal
    d. because they are primitive

82. The author says that sponges are "doing something right" because they . . .
    a. are strikingly beautiful.
    b. are preferred over synthetics.
    c. might be used against cancer.
    d. have existed for centuries.

83. The author mentions the lack of mouth and digestive cavity of sponges to show that sponges . . .
    a. are primitive.
    b. are multicellular.
    c. are animals.
    d. are zoophytes.

84. One can infer from the passage that the traditional use for sponges was to use them . . .
    a. for bathing.
    b. for medicine.
    c. for decoration.
    d. for laboratory study.

85. According to the passage, before the 19th century, sponges were erroneously believed to be . . .
    a. just barely animals.
    b. both plant and animal.
    c. both vertebrate and invertebrate.
    d. single-celled.

Until recently, because of the difficulty of testing hearing in small children, deafness often wasn't detected until a child was about two, too late to prevent a permanent language handicap. Now, however, there is a method to test infants' hearing by measuring electrical activity generated by the brain stem in response to sound. Through earphones, an infant is presented with a series of clicking sounds that stimulate the auditory nervous system. The electrical activity thus evoked in the brain is in turn picked up by electrodes placed behind each ear. These electrical signals are amplified, fed into a computer and printed out as waves on a graph. Within 12.5 milliseconds of a click, the graph of a normal baby will show seven distinct peaks, each representing a point along the path the sound has taken from the auditory nerve to the hearing centers of the cortex. For a baby with impaired hearing, the peaks take longer to appear. Different types of hearing defects, moreover, will produce wave patterns that deviate from the normal in characteristic ways. For example, absence of all seven waves indicates total sensory-neural deafness, usually untreatable. In conductive deafness, which can be treated, wave patterns will emerge if the intensity of the sound is increased.

86. The graph suggests that an infant's hearing problem can be helped if . . .
    a. no peaks appear on the graph.
    b. the waves are longer than the waves of normal infants.
    c. waves appear in less than 12.5 milliseconds of a click.
    d. waves only appear when the clicking sounds are made louder.

87. What is the function of the electrodes mentioned in the paragraph?
    a. They transmit the clicks to the computer.
    b. They detect the clicking sounds.
    c. They detect electrical activity in the brain.
    d. They stimulate the auditory nervous system.

88. What test results occur when an infant's hearing problem cannot be helped?
    a. No waves appear on the graph.
    b. The wave patterns are longer than those of a normal infant.
    c. The peaks on the graph are irregularly spaced.
    d. Peaks appear only when the intensity of the sound increases.

89. What is the function of the computer in this test?
    a. It sends electrical signals through the earphones.
    b. It transforms electrical signals into a printed pattern.
    c. It transforms electrical signals into sounds.
    d. It amplifies electrical signals.

90. According to the passage, why is this hearing test such an important development?
    a. It is more accurate than any other hearing test.
    b. It can be used on babies.
    c. It is not difficult to learn to administer the test.
    d. It is not difficult to learn to interpret the test.

Many 19th-century illusionists brought to their profession a zestful appetite for science. Most were grounded in ancient varieties of sleight of hand, and combined them with such specialities as juggling, ventriloquism, or mind reading. But they also found, in that century of prolific invention, that every new scientific invention had magic possibilities. The magician made it his business to stay a step or two ahead of public understanding of science.

The magic lantern had been used for private entertainment by the well-to-do in the 17th century, but late in the 18th century it suddenly acquired a virtuoso role in public entertainment. The genius behind this development was a Belgian experimenter, Etienne Robert. In 1797, when he acquired an abandoned chapel, surrounded by ancient tombs, on the grounds of an old Parisian monastery, he scored a historic success. Audiences entered through cavernous corridors, marked with strange symbols, and came on a dimly lit chamber decorated with skulls; effects of thunder, sepulchral music, and tolling bells helped to set the mood. Coal burned in braziers. Robert gave a preliminary discourse, denouncing charlatans and their bogus apparitions and promising something superior. He tossed some chemicals on the braziers, causing columns of smoke to rise. The single lamp flickered out, putting the audience in almost total darkness. Then, onto the smoke arising from the braziers, images were projected from his concealed magic lanterns. They included human forms and unearthly spectral shapes. The images came from glass slides, but the movements of the smoke gave them a ghoulish kind of life. Some spectators sank to their knees, convinced they were in the presence of the supernatural.

91. The main idea of this passage is that . . .
    a. magic can be used to explain scientific principles.
    b. magicians used advanced scientific knowledge to produce "magic."
    c. magic shows were very popular in the 17th century.
    d. magic is beyond the comprehension of the ordinary person.

92. According to the author, what did 19th-century magicians combine to produce their magic effects?
    a. mysterious sights and sounds
    b. mind reading and the supernatural
    c. superior intelligence and a gullible public
    d. skills and scientific knowledge

93. What made the images mentioned in the passage move?
    a. The glass slides moved back and forth.
    b. The magic lantern moved back and forth.
    c. They were projected onto moving smoke.
    d. They changed as the film moved through the projector.

94. How did Robert use the magic lantern?
    a. to decorate the chamber
    b. to project images
    c. to burn the chemicals
    d. to provide light in the room

95. The author uses Etienne Robert in this passage as an example of . . .
    a. a charlatan who used bogus apparitions.
    b. a gifted controller of the supernatural.
    c. an unrecognized scientific genius.
    d. a magician who used popularly unknown scientific techniques.

Some people dry mushrooms for winter use, and some can them. From my experience, I've found that freezing them produces erratic results: some species freeze well, while others do not. This is an area for experimentation on the part of each collector. Generally speaking, those forms like the brick cap, which fruit late in the fall, preserve fairly well by the deep-freeze technique.

Drying mushrooms, however, is one of the best ways of preserving them. Good circulation of warm air around the actual pieces being dried is the most important principle to be remembered here. But the specimens should not be overheated to the point that the tissue collapses and becomes wet. Since overheating almost always takes place if drying is done in an oven, the preferred method is to use a set of screens arranged one above the other. A sheet of flame-proofed canvas should be wrapped around it to obtain the effect of a chimney, and a hot plate placed at the bottom and used to provide steady heat. Steady heat is a cardinal point, since if the specimens are allowed to cool off when partly dried they become soggy and are not as good when finally dried out completely. When the pieces of mushroom on the screens have become crisp, they should be removed and stored in moisture-proof and insect-proof glass jars. To save space, only carefully cleaned, solid young mushrooms should be dried. As dried mushrooms mold very readily under conditions of high humidity and can become infested with the larvae of small beetles, the above-mentioned precautions are very important.

96. According to the author, what happens if the source of heat isn't constant?
    a. The mushrooms don't dry thoroughly.
    b. The mushrooms become overheated.
    c. The mushrooms expand and waste space.
    d. The mushrooms become insect-infested.

97. What does the author say about freezing mushrooms?
    a. Freezing preserves all mushrooms fairly well.
    b. Freezing is the best way to keep mold from spoiling the mushrooms.
    c. Freezing works well for only certain types of mushrooms.
    d. Freezing is the best way to take the moisture out of mushrooms.

98. The author uses the brick cap as an example of . . .
    a. a deep-freeze technique.
    b. a collector's experiment.
    c. a late-fruiting mushroom.
    d. a mushroom preserver.

99. What can be done to protect dried mushrooms from mold and larvae?
    a. Mushrooms must be stored in moisture- and insect-proof glass jars.
    b. Only solid, young, carefully cleaned mushrooms must be used.
    c. Steady heat must be maintained when drying the mushrooms.
    d. The mushrooms must be dried very carefully and completely.

100. According to the author, the most important part in the drying procedure is . . .
    a. putting the mushrooms in a hot oven.
    b. circulation of warm air around the mushrooms.
    c. cooling the mushrooms at the right time.
    d. storing the mushrooms in moisture- and insect-proof jars.

End Practice Test 1

## ■ PART 3: GRAMMAR, CLOZE, VOCABULARY, READING—PRACTICE TEST 2

**INSTRUCTIONS:** Do not begin this test until the examiner has read these instructions with you.

1.  Fill in the correct form on your answer sheet.

2.  This test contains 100 problems. There are four kinds: grammar, cloze, vocabulary, and reading comprehension. Examples of each kind of problem are given below.

3.  Each problem in the test has **only one** correct answer. Use a number 2 (soft) pencil to mark answers on the answer sheet. Make only one mark on your answer sheet for each problem. If you want to change an answer, completely erase the old mark.

4.  **Do not make any marks in this test booklet.** Write only on your answer sheet.

5.  The examiner will not explain any test problem; only the examples may be explained if you do not understand the problems.

6.  You will have 75 minutes to finish the entire test. Try to answer all the problems. Each problem counts the same. Do not spend too much time on any one problem or you will not have time to finish the test. Unanswered problems will be counted wrong. You may answer the problems in any order you wish.

7.  Here are examples of each kind of problem. In each example, the correct answer has been marked with an asterisk (*). For the actual problems, fill in the circle corresponding to the answer you choose. **Do not write in this test booklet.**

**GRAMMAR:** Choose the word or phrase that correctly completes the conversation.

> I.  "What is that thing?"
>     "That _____ a spider."
>     a.  to call
>     b.  for calling
>     c.  be called
>     *d.  is called

**CLOZE:** Read the passage, then select the word that best fills the blank in both grammar and meaning.

> Long ago, roads were only trails for people and animals to walk on, but today roads must be made for cars, trucks, and buses. The most modern _____ is often called a superhighway.
>
> II.  a.  way          *b.  road          c.  travel          d.  superhighway

**VOCABULARY:** Choose the word or phrase that correctly completes the sentence.

III. Because of the storm and rough waves, it
would be foolish to go out sailing today in
a small _____.
   a. automobile
   b. house
   *c. boat
   d. beast

**READING:** Read the passage, then answer the questions following it according to the information given in the passage.

**While I was getting ready to go to town one morning last week, my wife handed me a little piece of red cloth and asked if I would have time during the day to buy her two yards of cloth like that.**

IV. The person telling the story is . . .
   a. a married lady.
   b. an unmarried lady.
   *c. a married man.
   d. an unmarried man.

8.  Remember, you have 75 minutes (one hour and 15 minutes) to finish the entire test. Do not write in the test booklet. Mark only on the answer sheet. You may begin now.

## Part 3, Practice Test 2

For Problems 1 through 30, choose the word or phrase that correctly completes the sentence.

1. "Have you ever been to Hawaii?"
   "No, but I've thought about _____ there."
   a. going
   b. go
   c. to go
   d. will go

2. "Do you mind if people use your car?"
   "Not really, but it _____ that I'm getting tired of it."
   a. so often happens
   b. too often happens
   c. happens so often
   d. happens too often

3. "Can you meet me for lunch today?"
   "Yes, I _____ time to finish my housework by noon."
   a. will be having
   b. have had
   c. had
   d. will have had

4. "Professor Smith is very young."
   "Perhaps that is true, but she is _____ the most intelligent teacher in the university."
   a. moreover
   b. too
   c. even
   d. nonetheless

5. "Were you able to save anything from the fire?"
   "No, it happened so fast _____ anything we could do."
   a. that wasn't
   b. there wasn't
   c. wasn't
   d. it wasn't

6. "Do you eat in restaurants often?"
   "Not _____ I used to."
   a. as much as
   b. so much
   c. so much that
   d. as much

7. "Where should I put this dirty shirt?"
   "The clothing _____ is next to the washing machine."
   a. to be laundered
   b. for laundered
   c. laundering
   d. of laundering

8. "Do I have to apply for a new library card every year?"
   "No, your card is good for a _____ period."
   a. two years
   b. two year
   c. of two years
   d. two of years

9. "I thought the convention was always in March."
   "Usually it is, but next year it _____ in April."
   a. will hold
   b. is held
   c. will being holding
   d. is being held

10. "Did Betty and Donna sell many tickets?"
    "Yes, _____ the two of them, they sold nearly 100."
    a. besides
    b. by
    c. between
    d. for

11. "Was the concert held last night?"
    "No, it was called _____ because of the storm."
    a. off
    b. down
    c. out
    d. over

12. "The store manager called about your order."
    "When _____ shipped?"
    a. did he say was it
    b. he said it was
    c. did he say it was
    d. it was he did say

13. "Are typing and shorthand required for the job?"
    "Yes, those and _____ skills are necessary."
    b. other
    a. others
    c. another
    d. anothers

14. "Why aren't you washing the clothes?"
    "All the soap _____ up two days ago."
    a. was used
    b. has used
    c. have used
    d. used

15. "How was summer school?"
    "I took several interesting courses _____."
    a. which were also useful
    b. of which were useful too
    c. and as well useful
    d. and useful too

16. "How long will the potatoes take?"
    "They should _____ for at least an hour."
    a. baked
    b. bakes
    c. be bake
    d. bake

17. "You seem bored."
    "I am. I've done _____ sit around the house all day."
    a. nothing than
    b. nothing but
    c. none else but
    d. not else but

18. "Are Karen and Sue good friends?"
    "Yes, they _____ each other for years."
    a. have been knowing
    b. are knowing
    c. have known
    d. know

19. "Joe was told to leave the party."
    "I'm not surprised. His rude behavior wasn't _____."
    a. suitable
    b. suiting
    c. suited
    d. suitably

20. "Why is John so late?"
    "He had _____ a phone call."
    a. stopping to make
    b. to stop making
    c. to stop to make
    d. stopping making

21. "Do you need any help?"
    "No, I want to do this myself, and not let somebody else _____ for me."
    a. do it
    b. to do
    c. to do it
    d. do

22. "Do you know that girl?"
    "Yes, but I can't remember _____."
    a. from where do I know her
    b. where do I know her from
    c. where from I know her
    d. where I know her from

23. "What musical instruments do you play?"
    "I studied violin as a child, but now I _____ almost everything."
    a. am forgetting
    b. have forgotten
    c. do forget
    d. forget

24. "Did you hear that David got a video recorder?"
    "No. _____, we would have come right over."
    a. Had we known
    b. Were we known
    c. If we know
    d. Did we know

25. "Coffee is bad for your body."
    "Yes, I really must stop _____ it every day."
    a. drinking
    b. to drink
    c. drink
    d. drunk

26. "Did you hear his plan?"
    "Yes, _____ clever ideas he has."
    a. which
    b. that
    c. how
    d. what

27. "Is it hard to build a birdhouse?"
    "That depends on who is _____."
    a. doing the build
    b. doing the building
    c. done the building
    d. done the build

28. "Do you have any red pencils?"
    "No, they're _____ black."
    a. some
    b. scarcely
    c. mostly
    d. a few

29. "Please come to visit me tonight."
    "OK, I'll stop by your house, _____ it's late."
    a. even so
    b. even
    c. even that
    d. even if

30. "That's not the best way to do that."
    "How else _____?"
    a. can it be doing
    b. it can be done
    c. it can be doing
    d. can it be done

For Problems 31 through 50, choose the word that best fits each blank both in grammar and in meaning.

Drugs, despite their seemingly magical contributions to human health and comfort, have always been a mixed blessing. They have a capacity for great __(31)__ as well as great benefit; they __(32)__ be formulated and used carefully __(33)__ knowledgeably. Modern pharmaceutical scientists stress the need __(34)__ unremitting research to take the magic—and __(35)__ the uncertainty—out of the action __(36)__ drugs. One of their major __(37)__ is how to formulate a drug __(38)__ that it will work at the __(39)__ speed at the proper site in __(40)__ body without harming the patient in __(41)__ way.

Several researchers at the University of Michigan have been working on this __(42)__, and closely related questions, for several __(43)__ and within the framework of a __(44)__ of long term projects. Their basic __(45)__ is to find the best dosage __(46)__ any given drug and to be __(47)__ to predict its activity so precisely __(48)__ the proper regimen can be prescribed __(49)__ achieve optimal positive and __(50)__ negative effects. In this way, the accumulated knowledge of the pharmaceutical scientist serves as a tool for the physician.

| | | |
|---|---|---|
| 31. a. loss | c. advantage | |
| b. care | d. harm | |
| 32. a. could | c. would | |
| b. must | d. used | |
| 33. a. and | c. also | |
| b. with | d. very | |
| 34. a. to | c. for | |
| b. and | d. in | |
| 35. a. harm | c. thus | |
| b. use | d. not | |
| 36. a. of | c. toward | |
| b. from | d. any | |
| 37. a. discoveries | c. concerns | |
| b. abilities | d. actions | |
| 38. a. beneficial | c. composition | |
| b. besides | d. so | |
| 39. a. most | c. high | |
| b. rate | d. best | |
| 40. a. the | c. sick | |
| b. human | d. patient | |
| 41. a. other | c. several | |
| b. wrong | d. any | |
| 42. a. problem | c. field | |
| b. respect | d. theory | |
| 43. a. times | c. fields | |
| b. years | d. without | |
| 44. a. success | c. variety | |
| b. work | d. problem | |
| 45. a. foundation | c. item | |
| b. goal | d. look | |
| 46. a. to | c. than | |
| b. for | d. against | |
| 47. a. used | c. made | |
| b. tested | d. able | |
| 48. a. that | c. why | |
| b. as | d. and | |
| 49. a. as | c. that | |
| b. to | d. for | |
| 50. a. positive | c. also | |
| b. optimal | d. minimal | |

For Problems 51 through 80, chose the word or phrase that correctly completes the sentence.

51. He tried to _____ the money under a pile of boxes so that no one would find it.
    a. denote
    b. trace
    c. obstruct
    d. conceal

52. They don't report scores on each section of the test; they just add them all up and give the _____ score.
    a. compressed
    b. sequential
    c. aggregate
    d. intermediate

53. Tom's pretty forgiving; he doesn't hold a _____.
    a. grudge
    b. trait
    c. friction
    d. residue

54. The nurse could tell by his _____ face that he was sick with a fever.
    a. distinct
    b. flushed
    c. giddy
    d. husky

55. Businesses need to know the hard facts, like profit and loss, but they're also interested in the _____, like customer satisfaction.
    a. accessories
    b. intuitions
    c. compassions
    d. intangibles

56. The manager said that in his _____, the work could be finished in six months.
    a. apprehension
    b. manifestation
    c. estimation
    d. probation

57. Tom likes a lot of fruits; for example, he's very _____ to oranges and bananas.
    a. distinctive
    b. partial
    c. irresistible
    d. discreet

58. We'll have to _____ if we expect to get there on time.
    a. spark
    b. banter
    c. clinch
    d. hustle

59. Bill helped a lot. He was _____ in getting the job done.
    a. distinctive
    b. instrumental
    c. negotiable
    d. qualitative

60. The team has been very successful this year. Right now, they have a twenty game winning _____.
    a. streak
    b. spike
    c. clash
    d. punch

61. The engineers hoped the seawall would be able to _____ the force of the waves.
    a. withstand
    b. undermine
    c. uphold
    d. overturn

62. The driver brought the car to _____ stop.
    a. a rousing
    b. a brisk
    c. an abrupt
    d. an offensive

63. There is one _____ within the faculty of that department that always disagrees with the chairman.
    a. faction
    b. excerpt
    c. embodiment
    d. nomenclature

64. Alex _____ himself for the bad news.
    a. persisted
    b. braced
    c. resisted
    d. certified

65. Will the information the professor gave you be _____ to write the report?
    a. sufficient
    b. precise
    c. definitive
    d. eminent

66. The loose powder was _____ into a small container.
    a. compressed
    b. descended
    c. intensified
    d. resolved

67. Many apples are grown every year in that large _____ over there.
    a. provision
    b. cultivation
    c. harvest
    d. orchard

68. Be careful; this patient's disease is _____.
    a. congenial
    b. accessible
    c. compulsory
    d. contagious

69. The hot, dry weather caused the tomato plants to _____.
    a. stifle
    b. shutter
    c. wither
    d. crouch

70. Beth gave half of the money to her parents, but she kept the _____.
    a. remainder
    b. overthrow
    c. particle
    d. remnant

71. This book isn't printed clearly; everything is _____.
    a. biased
    b. blurred
    c. giddy
    d. filtered

72. At first, Charles said he'd never move to Alaska, but now he seems _____ to the idea.
    a. narrowed
    b. destined
    c. resigned
    d. indulged

73. The accident happened because the driver was blinded by the _____ of the setting sun.
    a. gaze
    b. streak
    c. glare
    d. splash

74. I didn't like the way the job was being done, so I used an _____ approach.
    a. alternative
    b. auxiliary
    c. approximate
    d. ambiguous

75. He cut his feet climbing up on the sharp, _____ rocks.
    a. stuffed
    b. jagged
    c. limp
    d. grizzly

76. Because we will never agree about this, any further discussion is _____.
    a. discernible
    b. heedless
    c. futile
    d. reflective

77. Harold came to the _____ that Larry had lied.
    a. standpoint
    b. outcome
    c. result
    d. conclusion

78. Susan and Jane had to share the prize because they finished the race _____.
    a. overwhelmingly
    b. simultaneously
    c. profoundly
    d. exclusively

79. Although I disagree with Joan, I try to be _____ her opinions.
    a. animated towards
    b. tolerant of
    c. resigned to
    d. callous about

80. She said he hadn't arrived yet, but that she expected him _____.
    a. momentously
    b. monumentally
    c. minutely
    d. momentarily

For Problems 81 through 100, read the passages, and then answer the questions following them according to the information given in the passage.

The record of people's manipulation of nature in the Florida Everglades is replete with examples of remedies that were never fully analyzed before they were applied—remedies that inevitably turned out to be more disastrous than the troubles they were intended to cure. It was people's judgment, for example, that the rich muck of South Florida was going to waste under water; so people drained off the water only to discover that muck, exposed to the heat of the sun, oxidizes into thin air. In some agricultural districts now as much as 40 percent of the organic soils are gone. Some farmers will be ploughing limestone in a few years. But they won't be raising any crops. Similarly, drainage undertaken to increase food production in one area has inhibited productivity in another; in periods of drought, the long canals became arms of the sea and salt water intruded on the land. In 1945, salinity in the soil killed off 18,000 acres of vegetables in southeast Dade county. Now increasing salinity in Florida Bay, caused by the decreasing outflow of fresh water from the Everglades, threatens the natural offshore nursery ground of the Tortugas shrimp and a $20 million annual commercial fishery.

81. One can infer from the passage that the canals were constructed in order to . . .
    a. reduce the danger of flooding.
    b. improve transportation.
    c. increase crop productivity.
    d. provide an entrance to the sea.

82. According to the passage, the canals allowed . . .
    a. the limestone to be exposed to air.
    b. seawater to drain from the land.
    c. seawater to enter farmlands.
    d. the prevention of floods.

83. According to the passage, what do Tortugas shrimp require in their nurseries?
    a. some fresh water mixed with the salt water
    b. a heavy concentration of salt water
    c. rapidly moving water
    d. a high, steady water temperature

84.  Seawater is found in the canals when . . .
   a.  there is a dry spell.
   b.  there is a flood.
   c.  the fresh water is diverted elsewhere.
   d.  the organic soils are gone.

85.  Why was the water drained off the muck?
   a.  to reduce the salinity in the soil
   b.  so the muck would oxidize
   c.  so the water could be used
   d.  so the muck could be used

The worldwide consumption of bakery products is increasing. Many populations that formerly relied solely on rice or coarser grains as their main source of carbohydrates show a preference for compounded bakery products as new industry and increased incomes make them more widely accessible. Japan is an outstanding example of countries following this trend. The United States has shown a steady downward trend in per capita consumption of cereal-based foods for many years, and the consumption of sweet bakery foods, such as cakes or pastry, has been increasingly displacing bread consumption.

Probably 95% of the white bread sold in the United States is enriched with thiamine, niacin, riboflavin, and iron, and about 30 of the 50 states have laws requiring white bread enrichment. Formerly, calcium and vitamin D were frequently added to enriched bread, but lack of consumer demand and questionable nutritional benefit led to gradual phasing out of these enrichments. India has attempted to encourage consumption of protein-enriched bread, with some success. Except for research projects, little has been done in other countries, however. In areas where bakery products comprise a large proportion of the diet, they could provide an ideal vehicle for nutritional supplementation. The need for better quality protein in the daily diet occurs mostly in the developing countries, where carbohydrate foods—usually cereals—are the basic components of the diet and therefore the logical protein carriers.

86. The main idea of the passage is that there is a worldwide trend toward . . .
    a. enriching the nutritional value of bread.
    b. using grains, such as rice, as a source of carbohydrates.
    c. increasing the consumption of protein.
    d. using bakery products as a source of carbohydrates.

87. According to the passage, in developing countries where there is heavy consumption of carbohydrate foods . . .
    a. protein enrichment of bread is not needed to supplement the diet.
    b. calcium and vitamin D are often added to supplement the diet.
    c. laws requiring white bread enrichment are needed.
    d. carbohydrate foods are ideal carriers for nutritional supplements.

88. Because of little demand and questionable value . . .
    a. calcium and vitamin D are no longer added to bread.
    b. cereal-based foods are being replaced by bakery products.
    c. little has been done to encourage consumption of enriched bread.
    d. rice and coarser grains are being replaced by bakery products.

89. Japan is used in this passage to illustrate a trend in many countries . . .
    a. to increase a reliance on rice and grains.
    b. to increase consumption of bakery foods.
    c. to enrich bread.
    d. to make industry more accessible.

90. In developing countries, popular cereals could be the best way to . . .
    a. increase reliance on carbohydrates.
    b. supplement the diet.
    c. encourage research projects.
    d. phase out necessary bread enrichments.

One of medicine's fundamental beliefs about pregnancy and the development of the human fetus has been challenged. Until recently, it was thought that the fetus was a parasite capable of extracting all the nutrients it needed from the mother. It is now realized that adequate nutrition during the entire course of the pregnancy is necessary for proper fetal development.

In early pregnancy, certain changes occur in the mother's gastrointestinal tract, resulting in more efficient absorption of specific nutrients, such as iron and calcium. Furthermore, the maternal blood supply increases, so that nutrients can be transported via the uterine and placental blood systems. If the mother is undernourished, this "lifeline" to the fetus will be inadequately developed. Finally, fat is accumulated within the body to store the energy necessary for lactation (milk production). This preparation for lactation is so important that if the mother is inadequately nourished, it will take place even at the expense of fetal growth. It is a logical developmental occurrence, since in the natural world, no infant can survive without successful breastfeeding, and thus fetal growth is less of a priority.

91. The main point of the passage is a discussion of . . .
    a. how the human fetus develops.
    b. methods of achieving proper maternal nutrition.
    c. the benefits of breastfeeding.
    d. the effect of maternal nutrition on the fetus.

92. What is required for lactation?
    a. increased blood supply
    b. iron and calcium
    c. fat storage
    d. a well-nourished placenta

93. What is the "lifeline" mentioned in the passage?
    a. the gastrointestinal tract
    b. breast feeding
    c. accumulated fat
    d. uterine and placental blood systems

94. What takes precedence over fetal growth?
    a. preparation for lactation
    b. fetal fat accumulation
    c. successful breastfeeding
    d. parasitic capabilities of the fetus

95. According to the passage, what traditional belief has been questioned?
    a. The fetus grows at the expense of the mother.
    b. Good nutrition is necessary throughout pregnancy.
    c. The mother's nourishment is more important than the baby's.
    d. The most important changes occur in early pregnancy.

Monticello ("little mountain") in Virginia is the estate and residence once owned by Thomas Jefferson, third president of the United States. Jefferson inherited the property in 1757 on the death of his father, Peter Jefferson, who in 1735 was given a government grant for this 1000 acre tract south of the Rivanna River, and who had subsequently acquired from a friend 400 additional acres for a homesite north of the Rivanna. Jefferson began having the mountaintop leveled for his homesite in 1768. There being no competent architect in the colonies to carry out his instructions, he mastered architecture by the study of books and drew his own plans, deriving his principal inspiration from the works of the Italian architect Andrea Palladio (1518–1580). Begun in 1769, the residence was developed in intermittent stages as its busy master found opportunity to return to it from his wanderings on the political and diplomatic scene, and it did not reach completion until after he left the presidency in 1809. He began occupying it in February 1770, after his paternal home at Shadwell, north of the Rivanna, had been destroyed by fire. The entire residence is one of the finest examples of the classical revival style, of which Jefferson was the first exponent in America.

96. Why did Thomas Jefferson study architecture?
    a. He wanted to help the architect design Monticello.
    b. He couldn't find an architect capable of designing his house.
    c. His father wanted him to study it.
    d. He wished to improve the buildings at Shadwell.

97. According to the passage, the original house at Shadwell was . . .
    a. designed by Peter Jefferson.
    b. built in the classical revival style.
    c. destroyed by fire, then rebuilt.
    d. the home of Peter Jefferson.

98. Why did it take as long as it did to build the residence at Monticello?
    a. Thomas Jefferson was busy elsewhere.
    b. It was destroyed by fire during its construction.
    c. It wasn't necessary to hurry, as Shadwell was available as a residence.
    d. It took that long for Thomas Jefferson to master architecture.

99. Why is Thomas Jefferson associated with the classical revival style?
    a. He admired and advocated it.
    b. His buildings are the only examples of it in the U.S.
    c. He tried to replace it with a more purely American style.
    d. He popularized it after his father invented it.

100. Why did Thomas Jefferson move into Monticello when he did?
    a. It was finally completed.
    b. He finally retired from the presidency.
    c. The house at Shadwell burned down.
    d. His father died, leaving him the estate.

End Practice Test 2

# Part 4: Speaking

The speaking test (oral interview) is not automatically included in every MELAB administration, but it is required for some professional certification programs and for University of Michigan applicants. If you are applying at the graduate level to a university in the United States and want to be considered for a teaching assistantship in order to get financial aid, it is strongly recommended that you include the speaking test in your MELAB test. There is an additional fee for the interview.

The speaking test cannot be taken by itself; it must be taken in conjunction with the MELAB Parts 1, 2, and 3. You must bring a blank audiocassette tape with you to the test site. You will not receive an official speaking test score unless a recorded cassette of your interview is included with the rest of your test papers. This is for quality control purposes. The speaking examiners are all trained by ELI-UM, and the tapes of the speaking tests are available for review if there is any question about the procedure or score.

You will have a 10 to 15–minute conversation with the local examiner, who will rate your overall communicative language proficiency. The examiner will consider six salient (prominent, or noticeable) features in your speaking before giving you an overall score. These features include fluency, intelligibility, conversational development and comprehension, and vocabulary and grammar. Your ability to make your meaning clear and to respond appropriately will be considered, as well as your ability to elaborate and develop your ideas.

The examiner will ask you questions about your background and future plans, and your opinions on certain issues. The examiner might ask you to explain or describe in detail something about your field of specialization. For example:

What schools have you applied to in the United States/Canada?

How did you happen to choose that school?

What do you plan to study there?

What is your educational background?  Where did you graduate from (high school/college/university)?  What degrees do you already have?

How long does a master's degree program (in your field) take?

Have you had any personal contact with any of your future professors?

Have you applied for a teaching assistantship or fellowship?

What is your favorite subject in school?  What is your least favorite subject?

What do you like most about your current job?  What do you like least?

What do you plan to do if you become certified in your field (nursing, dentistry, etc.)

What do you plan to do if you are accepted into this job training program?

What exactly does a (mechanical engineer/art historian/registered nurse) do?

What changes have occurred in your field over the past 25 years?

How does the work of a (dentist/architect/electrical engineer/nurse/medical technician) of today differ from one of 25 years ago?

What are your long-range plans? What do you plan to do after you (finish your degree program/ become certified)?

You should try to give more than a simple "yes" or "no" answer to the examiner's questions. If you do not understand a question, do not be afraid to ask the examiner to repeat or rephrase it.

It is common to be nervous in oral interviews. The examiner knows this and will try to make you relaxed, so that you can do your best.

Possible scores for the oral interview are 4, 3, 2, and 1, with 4 being the highest. If the examiner thinks your spoken English is good for your level, but not strong enough to raise it to the next level, he or she may add a plus (+) to your score, for example: 3+. The average oral rating is 2+.

Here are some brief descriptions of the kind of language seen at each level.

4:   The examinee is a highly fluent user of English, is a very involved participant in the interaction, and employs native-like prosody (pronunciation and intonation) with few hesitations in speech.

3:   The examinee is quite fluent and interactive but has gaps in linguistic range and control that usually occur during topic elaboration. Active in the interaction.

2:   Talk is quite slow and vocabulary is limited, though the examinee can usually convey communicative intent. The examinee does not always understand the examiner.

1:   Talk consists mainly of isolated phrases and formulaic expressions, and there are many communication breakdowns between the examiner and examinee.

Appendix C shows the Speaking Test Rating Scale and complete descriptors.

# KEYS, SCRIPTS, AND COMMENTARY FOR PRACTICE TESTS

# Part 2 (Listening) Practice Test Keys, Scripts, and Commentary

## Key, Script, and Commentary for Part 2, Practice Test 1

Do not look at the key and script until you have taken the practice test. Then score your test using the key. Finally, review the practice test by playing the audio as you read the script. Do *not* look at the key or script until you have finished the entire test. You will only harm yourself by doing so.

## Key to Part 2, Practice Test 1

| | | | | |
|---|---|---|---|---|
| 1. a | 11. b | 21. c | 31. b | 41. b |
| 2. a | 12. a | 22. a | 32. a | 42. a |
| 3. b | 13. b | 23. c | 33. a | 43. a |
| 4. c | 14. a | 24. a | 34. b | 44. a |
| 5. a | 15. b | 25. c | 35. c | 45. c |
| 6. c | 16. c | 26. b | 36. b | 46. b |
| 7. a | 17. a | 27. c | 37. c | 47. a |
| 8. a | 18. b | 28. b | 38. b | 48. a |
| 9. b | 19. a | 29. c | 39. c | 49. c |
| 10. c | 20. c | 30. c | 40. a | 50. c |

## Script and Commentary for Part 2, Practice Test 1

This part contains what is actually recorded on the CD that accompanies this book. The CD includes all the instructions as well as the cue questions and statements. The CD does not include the answer choices. They are printed in the test booklet. The correct answers are marked with an asterisk (*). After each test problem, a short explanation is given.

## Part 2, Practice Test 1

**Voice 1 (1ST FEMALE):** Part 2, Listening Comprehension, Practice Test 1. This is a test of how well you understand spoken English. There are several kinds of problems. In the first kind of problem, you will hear a question, and you must choose, from the three answer choices printed in your test booklet, a reasonable answer to the question. For example, listen to the question and choose one of the answers below.

Example I: Listen to the question.

**Voice 2 (2ND FEMALE):** When's she going on vacation?
    a.  last week
  * b.  tomorrow
    c.  to England

**Voice 1:** The correct answer is *b. tomorrow* because the speaker asked, *When's she going on vacation?*

In the second kind of problem, you will hear a very short conversation. For this kind of problem, choose the answer that means about the same thing as what you heard. For example, listen to the conversation.

Example II: Listen to the conversation.

**Voice 3 (MALE):** That movie was pretty bad.
**Voice 2 (FEMALE):** It sure was!
    a.  She agrees that it was beautiful.
    b.  She disagrees that it wasn't good.
  * c.  She agrees that it wasn't good.

**Voice 1:** The correct answer is *c. She agrees that it wasn't good* because the speakers said . . .
    **Voice 3 (MALE):** That movie was pretty bad.
    **Voice 2 (FEMALE):** It sure was!

**Voice 1:**
Finally, you will hear one short talk, or lecture, and two short radio reports on unrelated topics. You will be able to take notes as you listen. You may write your notes on the separate note page. After you hear each segment, you will be asked some questions about it. Mark all your answers on the separate answer sheet. Do NOT write in your test booklet. Please be very quiet and listen carefully. No problem can be repeated. Do you have any questions?

Now we will begin Practice Test 1. Turn the page to Problem Number 1.

**Voice 1:** For Problems 1 through 15, you will hear a short question. Choose a reasonable answer to the question.

**Voice 1:** Number 1.
**Voice 2 (FEMALE):** How're they going to get there?

  * a.  In Sue's car.
   b.  Sue's parents are.
   c.  Before noon.

The word *how* is the key to this problem. It asks not who (choice b) or when (choice c), but how (by what means) they will get there.

**Voice 1:** Number 2.
**Voice 3 (MALE):** What would you like to do after dinner tonight?

  * a.  See a movie.
   b.  I'd like to.
   c.  Steak and potatoes.

The speaker asks about what to do. This needs an answer that contains a verb about doing something.

**Voice 1:** Number 3.
**Voice 2 (FEMALE):** Would the train between New York and Chicago be cheaper than the plane?

   a.  Yes, I've been there twice.
  * b.  No, it's about twice as expensive.
   c.  No, it takes twice as long.

*Cheaper than* should let you know that prices are being compared.

**Voice 1:** Number 4.
**Voice 3 (MALE):** When you were in the teacher's office, what were you talking about?

   a.  Not in the office.
   b.  At 2 o'clock.
  * c.  My last test.

The speaker wanted to know what was being talked about.

**Voice 1:** Number 5.
**Voice 2 (FEMALE):** Don't you want to go?

  * a.  Yes, I do.
   b.  No, she doesn't.
   c.  Yes, she will.

*Don't you* may sound like *don'she,* but it does require the listener to answer for himself/herself, rather than for the *she* in choices b and c.

**Voice 1:** Number 6.

**Voice 3 (MALE):** If you're having trouble with those scissors, why don't you use mine?

    a. Yes, you can use them.

    b. No, you don't.

   \* c. Because yours aren't any better.

To answer this, you need to give a reason why you won't use the speaker's scissors.

**Voice 1:** Number 7.

**Voice 2 (FEMALE):** I need to meet with you, but I work during your office hours. What can I do?

  \* a. Make a special appointment with me.

    b. My office is in Room 203.

    c. My office hours are from 9 to 11.

The speaker needs to know what to do, not where the office is located or when the regular office hours are.

**Voice 1:** Number 8.

**Voice 3 (MALE):** Do you want me to stay until you're finished?

  \* a. If you want to.

    b. No, I'm not.

    c. Yes, I'm finished.

This kind of question is not asking for information, but for an opinion. It is typical of conversational English. The speaker is being polite. The speaker wants to be told what to do. He knows the person he is talking to is not finished yet. Rather than telling exactly what to do, the correct answer leaves it up to the speaker to decide.

**Voice 1:** Number 9.

**Voice 2 (FEMALE):** What do you think about going to the movies with our neighbors tonight?

    a. Late last night.

  \* b. Sounds like fun.

    c. They'll go with you.

The key here is *what do you think?* The speaker is asking for an opinion about her suggestion for something to do.

**Voice 1:** Number 10.

**Voice 3 (MALE):** If it hadn't rained all last week, would the river have flooded?

    a. The river flooded.

    b. When it rained last night.

  \* c. It might have.

This is grammatically based: it is a negative conditional. We know from what the speaker said that it did rain last week and that the river did flood. The speaker is wondering what would have happened if it had not rained last week.

**Voice 1:** Number 11.
**Voice 2 (Female):** I'm going to be working in New York City next year. What's the most common way to get around?

    a. Near Central Park.
  * b. The subway.
    c. Straight down 5th Avenue.

*The most common way to get around* is an idiom, meaning the most usual means of transportation. It doesn't mean where it is or how to get to it.

**Voice 1:** Number 12.
**Voice 3 (Male):** Why didn't you have Fred get the papers?

  * a. He wasn't here.
    b. In order to get them.
    c. For the secretary.

The first part of the question, *Why didn't you,* may sound like *Why din't chew,* making it more difficult to understand. The question asks for a reason why a person (Fred) didn't do something.

**Voice 1:** Number 13.
**Voice 2 (Female):** Can you give me a hand with this work?

    a. I'll see if it works.
  * b. Sure, I can help.
    c. OK, give me one.

To *give someone a hand* is an idiom that means to help someone.

**Voice 1:** Number 14.
**Voice 3 (Male):** Did the police get any evidence from the crime scene?

  * a. Just some footprints.
    b. No, the thief got away.
    c. It was over when they got there.

This question requires that the listener knows what *evidence* is. Police collect material, such as footprints, fingerprints, or hair samples, as concrete proof (evidence) for investigations.

**Voice 1:** Number 15.
**Voice 2 (Female):** Could I borrow your lecture notes from the last class?

    a. OK, I'll borrow yours.
  * b. Sorry, I missed it too.
    c. It was the last one.

The speaker didn't go to the last class so is asking her classmate for the notes.

**Voice 1:** For Problems 16 through 35, you will hear short conversations. Choose the statement that means about the same thing as what you hear.

**Voice 1:** Number 16.

(**Male**): Uh oh. Is today the 21st?

(**Female**): Yeah, so?

(**Male**): I think I have a doctor appointment today.

(**Female**): Wait, let me check—no, you're safe; it's tomorrow.

     a.  He doesn't need to see the doctor.

     b.  He missed his appointment.

  * c.  He'll see the doctor the next day.

He's not sure of the date of the appointment and thinks he's missed it. She sees that the appointment is for the following day. *You're safe* doesn't mean he's not sick, just that he didn't miss the appointment.

**Voice 1:** Number 17.

(**Male**): I didn't see Jane at the party last night.

(**Female**): She was there, but she left early. You must've come later.

  * a.  Jane didn't stay late.

     b.  Jane came later.

     c.  Jane didn't go.

Jane was at the party but left before the man arrived.

**Voice 1:** Number 18.

(**Female**): Were you able to make a reservation at the restaurant?

(**Male**): They said they don't take reservations.

(**Female**): Oh well, we'll just have to get there early then.

     a.  They won't go.

  * b.  They'll go sooner.

     c.  They'll go somewhere else.

Since the restaurant won't reserve a table for them, they plan to arrive early so they can get a table.

**Voice 1:** Number 19.

(**Male**): I can't wait to see the big football match on TV!

(**Female**): Well, don't wait too long. It started an hour ago.

(**Male**): Yikes! Oh well, at least I'll see part of it.

  * a.  He missed the start.

     b.  He missed the whole match.

     c.  He'll wait to see it later.

The match is now underway, so he will be able to see the last part even though he missed the beginning.

**Voice 1:** Number 20.

(FEMALE): The Islamic exhibit at the art museum is fabulous!

(MALE): I've been meaning to go but haven't found the time.

(FEMALE): You'd better see it soon—it closes at the end of the week.

    a.  It's too late for him to go.

    b.  He's already gone.

  \* c.  He shouldn't delay any longer.

She has been to the exhibit, but he has not. He can still see it if he goes before the end of the week.

**Voice 1:** Number 21.

(MALE): Is this where I register for classes?

(FEMALE): No, you'll have to go to the office next door.

(MALE): But it's closed.

(FEMALE): They're probably at lunch. Come back after one o'clock.

    a.  He can't find the right office.

    b.  He should return to her office at 1:00.

  \* c.  He can register after 1:00.

They do not know each other. She works in an office near the registrar's office. He had gone to the right office for registration, but it was closed. She tells him he should go back to the registrar's office later.

**Voice 1:** Number 22.

(MALE): Are you taking Professor Morton's economics class this term?

(FEMALE): There are some prerequisites I have to get out of the way first.

  \* a.  She needs to take other classes first.

    b.  She needs to take Professor Morton's class first.

    c.  She already took Professor Morton's class.

*Prerequisites* are requirements (in this case, classes) that someone must take in advance, before taking the economics class.

**Voice 1:** Number 23.

(FEMALE): Are you having as much trouble following the chemistry lectures as I am?

(MALE): No, but I already covered a lot of the material in high school.

    a.  He's having trouble too.

    b.  He came sooner than she did.

  \* c.  He was better prepared.

He is already familiar with most of the material since he studied it before. The material is new and, therefore, difficult for her.

**Voice 1:** Number 24.

(FEMALE): I'm having a hard time starting this paper assignment.

(MALE): Why don't you start in the middle and do the introduction later?

    \* a.  He suggests a different order.

      b.  He thinks she works too hard.

      c.  He thinks she doesn't work hard enough.

He's making a suggestion about how to do the assignment, not about how hard she's working on it.

**Voice 1:** Number 25.

(FEMALE): Did Professor Steiner say when the final paper is due?

(MALE): The end of the month. But he did say we could get an extension.

      a.  They don't have to turn one in.

      b.  It must be turned in on time.

    \* c.  It can be turned in later.

The paper is due at the end of the month, but if students ask, they can get the due date *extended* to a later date.

**Voice 1:** Number 26.

(FEMALE): Mr. Brown, could I speak to you for a moment about the homework assignment?

(MALE): I've got another class right now. Why don't you come to my office hours this afternoon?

(FEMALE): Okay.

      a.  He'll talk to her now.

    \* b.  He'll talk to her later.

      c.  He won't talk to her.

She is his student. Mr. Brown doesn't have time to talk to her now, but he suggests that she come to his office later in the day.

**Voice 1:** Number 27.

(MALE): There was a car crash at the corner last night.

(FEMALE): I didn't know. Was anyone hurt?

(MALE): Yeah, not seriously though.

      a.  He wasn't badly injured.

      b.  Someone was badly injured.

    \* c.  No one was badly injured.

Someone was injured, but not badly. He was not in the crash, so he couldn't have been injured (choice a).

**Voice 1:** Number 28.

(**MALE**): Slow down! This is a 25 miles per hour zone.

(**FEMALE**): Stay out of it! I know what I'm doing.

(**MALE**): Okay, but remember you got a speeding ticket last time.

    a.  She wants him to get out of the car.

 * b.  He thinks she drives too fast.

    c.  He'll give her a ticket.

They're having an argument about her driving. When she says, *Stay out of it,* she means that she doesn't want him to criticize her, not that she wants him to get out of the car (choice a). He is a passenger, not a police officer who can give her a ticket (choice c).

**Voice 1:** Number 29.

(**MALE**): Wouldn't you know it! No sooner do I leave than I realize I've left my keys in the house.

(**FEMALE**): I've got a spare set you can use.

(**MALE**): But then you'll be without.

(**FEMALE**): That's okay, you'll be back before me.

    a.  They can't get back in the house.

    b.  They'll go back to get the keys.

 * c.  She has extra keys.

They have just left the house, and he has just remembered that he left his keys inside. She will let him use her keys. He will return before she does, and he can let her in the house then.

**Voice 1:** Number 30.

(**FEMALE**): Could you help me with these figures? I can't get them to add up right.

(**MALE**): Why don't you just borrow my calculator?

    a.  He can't do it either.

    b.  He will do it for her.

 * c.  She can use his calculator.

He won't add the figures for her (choice b) even though he is able to (choice a), but he will let her use his calculator to do it herself.

**Voice 1:** Number 31.

(**FEMALE**): I've had it with this computer! It keeps shutting down on me.

(**MALE**): Don't throw it out. Maybe it just needs some new parts.

(**FEMALE**): That's a possibility. I'll call the computer tech.

    a.  She'll buy a new one.

 * b.  She'll have it repaired.

    c.  He'll fix it for her.

He suggests that she have the computer repaired so that she won't have to buy a new one (choice a). Someone else (the computer technician) will fix it, not the male speaker (choice c).

**Voice 1:** Number 32.

(**Female**): Do you think Bob was serious about quitting his job?

(**Male**): Trust me. He was just blowing off steam. He doesn't have anything else lined up.

   * a.  He thinks Bob won't quit.
     b.  He thinks Bob will quit.
     c.  He thinks Bob has a new job.

They are both friends of Bob. When he says Bob was *blowing off steam,* he means Bob was complaining loudly. But he thinks Bob won't quit because Bob doesn't have anything else—another job.

**Voice 1:** Number 33.

(**Female**): Can you take over for me for a few minutes while I take a short break?

(**Male**): Sure, no problem.

   * a.  He'll replace her for a while.
     b.  He'll take it there for her.
     c.  He can fix the broken equipment.

Several colloquialisms are used here. *Take over* means to replace her or do her work while she's away. *A short break* means a brief time away from work, to rest. The man is willing to help her out by doing her work while she is away briefly.

**Voice 1:** Number 34.

(**Male**): What documents do we have to bring to registration?

(**Female**): Your identity card or school ID.

     a.  He doesn't need to take anything.
   * b.  He should take some identification.
     c.  She can register him now.

He is planning to register but won't do it now. She tells him what he needs to take when he registers.

**Voice 1:** Number 35.

(**Male**): I think I'd better leave. This discussion isn't getting us anywhere.

(**Female**): I couldn't agree more.

     a.  They think the discussion was useful.
     b.  They'll leave together.
   * c.  They're having an argument.

The speakers don't say directly what they mean. Sometimes *discussion* means an argument. They have been discussing something but can't agree, so the man has decided to leave. The woman agrees that their discussion has failed.

**Voice 1:** In the last part of the test, you will hear a short talk, or lecture, and two short radio reports on unrelated topics. As you listen, you may take notes on the separate note page. Do not write in this test booklet. When each segment is finished, you will be asked some questions about it. You may use your notes to answer the questions.

Now you will hear a short talk by an environmentalist.

**Voice 3:**
Pollution due to overpopulation is a problem in many of the world's developed countries. The northeast corner of the United States is no exception. On the northeast coast of the United States, bordering the Atlantic Ocean, there are many environmental problems related to pollution. There are many causes, but scientists say they are primarily due to land development and its consequence, overpopulation. Some of these pollution problems are quite obvious, while others aren't really noticeable to the general populace. Development has brought changes you can't ignore, like more houses, more boats, and more traffic jams. But there are other changes you can't see, changes in the marine environment that warn of problems.

At Woods Hole, Massachusetts, researchers at the Woods Hole Oceanographic Institute study the marine fauna—that is, sea animals. The researchers warn that signs of stressed environment are present. When examining a sample of the marine fauna, marine biologists have noticed that now there are fewer species as compared to 30 or 40 years ago. In some cases, there is only one single culture of one single species. The existence of only a single species is the big tip-off to a stressed environment, according to marine biologists. For example, there's the hardshell clam. It can live where other shellfish can't. But the hardshell clams at Woods Hole are so polluted that they can't be used for food, though they can be used as seed clams to populate shellfish beds elsewhere.

In some places the shellfish bed pollution is so bad and consequent bacteria counts have been so high that recreational swimming beaches have to be closed, and people are surprised. But they shouldn't be because the problem's been creeping up on them a house lot at a time. They've been continuing to develop new housing areas, which demand fresh water and sewage treatment.

This problem may now be worst in the northeast area, but it is also occurring in other parts of the United States that are also experiencing population growth.

**Voice 1:** End of the lecture. Now you will be asked some questions about it, Numbers 36 through 40. You may use any notes you have taken.

Number 36. What are the *visible* signs of development?
   a.  polluted water
 * b.  traffic jams, more houses and boats
   c.  fewer shellfish
In Paragraph 1, these were given as examples of *changes you can't ignore,* and they are visible. They are contrasted with *other changes you can't see,* choices a and c, which are talked about later in the lecture.

Number 37. What do marine biologists say is the key sign of a *stressed* environment?
    a. Water becomes polluted.
    b. Clams become polluted and can't be eaten.
  * c. The number of marine fauna species is reduced.
In Paragraph 2, *fewer species* is given as an example of a sign of a stressed environment. It's an important sign because the lecturer says it's *the big tip-off.* A *tip-off* is a clue to a puzzle or mystery. Choice a is the problem, not a sign of it, and choice b, the clam, is given as an example.

Number 38. According to the lecture, what is the original source of the pollution?
    a. high bacteria counts
  * b. land development
    c. a stressed environment
In the first paragraph, scientists say the environmental problems are primarily due to land development and overpopulation. Choices a and c are results, not causes, of pollution.

Number 39. What has happened to the hardshell clam at Woods Hole?
    a. It has died off.
    b. It can't be used as a seed clam.
  * c. It is so polluted it can't be eaten.
At the end of Paragraph 2, the lecturer says the clams are *so polluted they can't be used for food.* Choices a and b are not true; in both cases, the opposite is true.

Number 40. What happens to make people realize how polluted the marine environment is?
  * a. Beaches are closed to swimmers.
    b. Clams and fish have died off.
    c. The beachfront is crowded with houses and boats.
In Paragraph 3, the lecturer says the people are surprised when they find the beaches closed. You can infer (guess) that they were unaware of the problem until then. Choices b and c are wrong because the people don't realize the problem even when those things are happening.

**Voice 1:** Now you will hear the first short radio report.

**Voice 1 (ANNOUNCER):** Our reporter, Mark Smith, is interviewing a research psychologist who's interested in memory studies.

**Voice 2 (MALE REPORTER):** Today I'm interviewing Mary Browning, a psychologist who's been studying computer programs that claim to improve your memory.

**Voice 3 (FEMALE EXPERT):** We analyzed a lot of computer games that claimed to "train" or improve your brain, your memory. Not all of the programs worked, and for those that do, we don't really understand how and why. One problem is, the older a person is, and the less memory ability he or she has before training, the less likely that person is to show benefits. The bottom line is that the people who need the memory training the <u>most</u>—those 80 and older and people with lower initial ability—improve the <u>least</u>.

**Voice 2 (MALE REPORTER):** And why is that?

**Voice 3 (FEMALE EXPERT):** We found that the type of benefit that people get from memory training is related to the kinds of strategies people use. We took a memory training program and asked what was different about people who showed big benefits and those who didn't. The groups we looked at were healthy older adults and older adults at the beginning of Alzheimer's disease, which affects memory.

Participants in the study practiced memorizing material, then were tested on it. What we found was that the <u>strategies</u> are related to the benefit—that accounting for those <u>strategies</u> can eliminate age and abilities in training success. People in their 60s and 70s who used the strategy of spending most of their time on studying materials and very little time on the test itself showed big improvements over the testing sessions. In contrast, people in their 80s and older spent little time studying the materials and spent most of their time on the test. They didn't do well on the test, and they showed little improvement, even after two weeks of training.

**Voice 2 (MALE REPORTER):** So it looks like these results show that in order to improve memory, one needs not only to work <u>hard</u>, but also to work <u>smart</u>.

*Adapted from Joe Serwach, The University (of Michigan) Record, 2007.*

**Voice 1 (ANNOUNCER):** End of the interview. Now you will hear five questions about it, Numbers 41 through 45.

Number 41. What is the researcher studying?
    a. computer programmers' claims
  * b. methods of improving memory
    c. effects of aging on memory
This question asks about the main idea of the report. The expert is studying the effects of memory training on older adults.

Number 42. What process did the researcher follow in order to collect data?
  * a. Subjects were tested on material they had studied.
    b. Subjects practiced using a variety of strategies.
    c. Subjects analyzed computer games.
The researcher says, *participants in the study practiced memorizing material, then were tested on it.*

Number 43. What was the key to successful memory training?

  * a. using effective strategies
    b. using effective computer games
    c. using a variety of programs and strategies

The researcher emphasizes the relationship between the kinds of strategies people use and the relationship between these strategies and training success. Even though she says some of the computer programs worked (choices b and c), she isn't sure why, so she can't relate the programs to success.

Number 44. What happened to the people who needed the memory training the most?

    a. They didn't improve even with more training.
  * b. They improved the least.
    c. They improved the most.

The researcher says that the people who needed the training the most were the ones who improved the least. These were the oldest participants with Alzheimer's disease.

Number 45. What strategy did the most successful participants use?

    a. They concentrated on the best computer games.
    b. They concentrated on taking the test.
  * c. They concentrated on memorizing the material.

The researcher says the most successful participants in the study spent *most of their time on studying materials and very little time on the test itself.*

**Voice 1:** Now you will hear the second short radio report.

**Voice 1 (ANNOUNCER):** Our reporter, Carolyn Baker, reports on some new medical research.

**Voice 2 (FEMALE REPORTER):** Health care professionals are increasingly concerned about the overuse of antibiotics. As more and more antibiotic drugs are used, bacteria become resistant to them. We're speaking today with Dr. James Burghart, who is working with natural antibiotics—natural antibiotics produced by virtually all animals, from insects to frogs to humans. Dr. Burghart, can you explain how this works?

**Voice 3 (MALE EXPERT):** The natural antibiotics we're working with are compounds called Antimicrobial Peptides, or A-M-Ps, AMPs. AMPs are the body's immune system's first line of defense against bacteria. There's been interest in exploiting these natural antibiotics for 20 years, but the AMPs are easily broken down by natural enzymes in the body as well as by bacterial enzymes. The simple solution to that problem—merely increasing the concentration of AMPs—can cause toxic side-effects, like the destruction of red blood cells. That happens because sticky parts of the AMP molecule interact with the red blood cell's cell membrane in a harmful way.

**Voice 2 (Female Reporter):** Dr. Burghart, you said your team found a way to replace sticky parts of the AMPs with non-stick versions—similar to non-stick cookware, like Teflon®-coated pots and pans.

**Voice 3 (Male Expert):** Yes, we were inspired by Teflon®. Teflon cookware is coated with plastic compounds—plastic that has been treated with fluorine—which makes the coating slippery, rather than sticky. What we did was to replace the sticky parts of AMP molecules with non-stick, fluorinated versions. That made the AMP molecules resistant to the enzymes that were breaking them down. We compared plain AMPs with fluorinated AMPs. We found that the plain AMPs degraded in 30 minutes while the fluorinated AMPs were still intact after 10 hours. So this process of fluorinating the AMPs will make them more effective, since they'll stay around longer in the body. And though our research now has obvious practical applications, it started just as an exploration in basic science. We were just interested in translating useful properties of man-made materials into biological molecules. In the future, these fluorinated natural antibiotics might be used instead of conventional man-made antibiotics that bacteria are becoming resistant to.

**Voice 2 (Female Reporter):** So your basic research had an unanticipated beneficial outcome—it developed into an application for a very important clinical problem in medicine.
*Adapted from Nancy Ross-Flanigan, The University of Michigan News Service, 2007.*

**Voice 1 (Announcer):** Now you will hear five questions about the radio report, Numbers 46 through 50.

Number 46. How did the research start?
    a. as a study of the body's immune system
  \* b. as a study applying man-made to biological materials
    c. as a study of bacteria-resistant antibiotics
In the last segment, the researcher says, *it started just as an exploration in basic science,* that he was *just interested in translating useful properties of man-made materials into biological molecules.*

Number 47. Why are natural AMPs better than man-made antibiotics?
  \* a. Bacteria don't become resistant to AMPs.
    b. AMPs are not broken down by enzymes.
    c. AMPs are not toxic, even in large doses.
This is related to the medical problem being discussed, that bacteria are becoming resistant to man-made antibiotics. The researchers are hoping to replace man-made antibiotics with treated natural ones, AMPs. Choices b and c are false. Untreated AMPs are broken down by enzymes, and we can assume that both untreated and treated AMPs are toxic in large doses.

Number 48. What inspired the original research?

     \* a.  man-made cookware

     b.  bacteria resistant to antibiotics

     c.  interest in exploiting natural antibiotics

The researcher says, *We were inspired by Teflon,* and then he goes on to describe Teflon cookware. It was only later that his team saw how its research could be applied to medicine.

Number 49. What happens if plain natural AMPs are highly concentrated in the body?

     a.  They become less resistant to bacteria.

     b.  They become sticky.

     \* c.  They destroy red blood cells.

The researcher explains that the sticky parts of the untreated AMP molecules interact with the red blood cell's cell membrane, destroying it.

Number 50. Why are the fluorinated AMPs more effective than the plain AMPs?

     a.  They resist more kinds of bacteria.

     b.  They are more concentrated in the body.

     \* c.  They last longer in the body.

The fluorinated AMPs don't degrade, or break down, like the untreated AMPs do.

End of Practice Test 1

## Key, Script, and Commentary for Part 2, Practice Test 2

Do not look at the key and script for Part 2, Practice Test 2 until you have taken the practice test. Then score your test using the key. Finally, review the practice test by playing the tape recording as you read the script. Do *not* look at the key or script until you have finished the entire test. You will only harm yourself by doing so.

## Key to Part 2, Practice Test 2

| | | | | |
|---|---|---|---|---|
| 1. c | 11. b | 21. b | 31. a | 41. b |
| 2. b | 12. a | 22. b | 32. a | 42. a |
| 3. a | 13. c | 23. b | 33. b | 43. c |
| 4. a | 14. b | 24. c | 34. a | 44. b |
| 5. c | 15. a | 25. a | 35. c | 45. a |
| 6. a | 16. c | 26. c | 36. c | 46. c |
| 7. b | 17. a | 27. b | 37. b | 47. b |
| 8. c | 18. b | 28. c | 38. a | 48. c |
| 9. a | 19. c | 29. b | 39. c | 49. c |
| 10. a | 20. c | 30. b | 40. a | 50. a |

## Script and Commentary for Part 2, Practice Test 2

This part contains what is actually recorded on the CD that accompanies this book. The instructions consist of what is recorded on the CD. The examples and problems consist of what is recorded as well as the printed answer choices. The correct answers are marked with an asterisk (*). After each test problem, a short explanation is given.

## Part 2, Practice Test 2

**Voice 1 (1ST FEMALE):**
Part 2, Listening Comprehension, Practice Test 2. This is a test of how well you understand spoken English. There are several kinds of problems. In the first kind of problem, you will hear a question, and you must choose, from the three answer choices printed in your test booklet, a reasonable answer to the question. For example, listen to the question and choose one of the answers below.

Example I: Listen to the question.

**Voice 2 (2ND FEMALE):** When's she going on vacation?
    a. last week
 * b. tomorrow
    c. to England

**Voice 1:** The correct answer is *b. tomorrow* because the speaker asked, *When's she going on vacation?*

In the second kind of problem, you will hear a very short conversation. For this kind of problem, choose the answer that means about the same thing as what you heard. For example, listen to the conversation.

Example II: Listen to the conversation.

**Voice 3 (MALE):** That movie was pretty bad.
**Voice 2 (FEMALE):** It sure was!
    a. She agrees that it was beautiful.
    b. She disagrees that it wasn't good.
 * c. She agrees that it wasn't good.

**Voice 1:** The correct answer is *c. She agrees that it wasn't good* because the speakers said . . .

    **Voice 3 (MALE):** That movie was pretty bad.

    **Voice 2 (FEMALE):** It sure was!

**Voice 1:** Finally, you will hear one short talk, or lecture, and two short radio reports on unrelated topics. You will be able to take notes as you listen. You may write your notes on the separate note page. After you hear each segment, you will be asked some questions about it. Mark all your answers on the separate answer sheet. Do NOT write in your test booklet. Please be very quiet and listen carefully. No problem can be repeated. Do you have any questions?

Now we will begin Practice Test 2. Turn the page to Problem Number 1.

**Voice 1:** For Problems 1 through 15, you will hear a short question. Choose a reasonable answer to the question.

**Voice 1:** Number 1.
(**Male**): Where can I find Professor Johnson's office?
    a. No, I don't think you can.
    b. If you want to.
  * c. At the end of the hall.
He needs to know the location of the office.

**Voice 1:** Number 2.
(**Female**): When Tom comes home, do you think he'll give me a hand with the party decorations?
    a. Maybe he came to the party.
  * b. If he's not busy.
    c. Yes, he gave them to me.
The speaker is asking for an opinion in a hypothetical future situation. To *give someone a hand* means to help him or her to do something. She is asking if Tom can help her, and the appropriate reply shows that Tom can if he's not busy doing something else.

**Voice 1:** Number 3.
(**Male**): Do you think you'll be able to stop by the cleaners and get my coat on the way home from work tonight?
  * a. Sure, I'll do it.
    b. After I go to the cleaners.
    c. On my way home.
He is asking a favor of the listener—he wants the listener to get his coat from the cleaners. *Do you think you'll be able to* is a polite way of saying *please*.

**Voice 1:** Number 4.
(**Female**): What exactly does she disapprove of about this program?
  * a. It's hard to say.
    b. Yes, she can improve it.
    c. No, I can't prove it.
This question depends on your understanding of the word *disapprove,* which may sound like *improve* or *prove.* The speaker is asking what is disapproved of. Rather than telling exactly what, the answer shows uncertainty.

**Voice 1:** Number 5.

(**MALE**): How do you find life in the city?

    a.  I take the bus.

    b.  My brother told me how.

  * c.  I enjoy it.

*How do you find* in this context means "what is it like" or "what do you think about."

**Voice 1:** Number 6.

(**FEMALE**): Would you mind giving this to the teacher for me tomorrow?

  * a.  Sorry, I'm not going to class.

    b.  Sorry, I don't mind.

    c.  Yes, please give it to her.

The speaker is asking a favor: please give this to the teacher. *Would you mind* is a polite way of asking a favor. The response is a polite refusal; it is polite because it gives a good reason for not being able to do the favor.

**Voice 1:** Number 7.

(**FEMALE**): Do you think you can give me more help than you've been giving me lately?

    a.  Yes, Mary has.

  * b.  No, I can't.

    c.  Yes, it was late.

*Lately* means "recently." The speaker is asking the listener to help her more.

**Voice 1:** Number 8.

(**MALE**): If I'm having trouble, when can I come to your office?

    a.  Sure, no problem.

    b.  At my office.

  * c.  On Friday.

The speaker wants to know when he should come to the office for help, if he should need it.

**Voice 1:** Number 9.

(**FEMALE**): You know that secretarial job you have open—how much do you count for typing speed?

  * a.  It's quite important.

    b.  50 words per minute.

    c.  Open it quickly.

That the job is *open* means that it is available, that the company wants to hire someone to fill the position. The speaker wants to know how important it is to be a fast typist in order to get the job.

**Voice 1:** Number 10.

(**MALE**): Do you think I should finish writing this, or go to the store first?

    \* a. Do the writing first.

    b. Both of them will.

    c. OK, I'll go there first.

The speaker is asking for an opinion. He wants someone to decide for him which thing he should do first.

**Voice 1:** Number 11.

(**FEMALE**): How's the paper coming along?

    a. Sure, I'll come.

    \* b. It's nearly finished.

    c. When you're ready.

The speaker is asking about the progress that is being made in writing a paper.

**Voice 1:** Number 12.

(**MALE**): Can you justify your opinion about the influence of the military?

    \* a. I have two reasons.

    b. That's my opinion.

    c. They caused it.

The speaker is asking for reasons to support the listener's opinion, not what the opinion is (choice c).

**Voice 1:** Number 13.

(**FEMALE**): John and Sue are going at it again. I wonder if you could intervene.

    a. They can if they want to.

    b. They haven't stopped yet.

    \* c. Let them settle it by themselves.

This is not a direct question but a request for assistance. *Going at it* means John and Sue are arguing, and the speaker wants the listener to stop them. The response (choice c) shows that the listener doesn't want to intervene but feels they should make peace by themselves.

**Voice 1:** Number 14.

(**MALE**): Do you think I can transfer my credits from the college to another university?

    a. It's in the records.

    \* b. Sure, it's done all the time.

    c. If you put them there.

The speaker is a student at a college and wants to get credit for courses he's taken at a different university.

**Voice 1:** Number 15.

(**Female**): Were they able to isolate the cause of the disease?

    * a. They found two possibilities.

      b. They were alone.

      c. That's the cause.

To *isolate* the cause means "to find a single source." The answer shows that there were two possible causes.

**Voice 1:** For Problems 16 through 35, you will hear short conversations. Choose the statement that means about the same thing as what you hear.

**Voice 1:** Number 16.

(**Female**): I can't find my keys, and I've been looking all over.

(**Male**): I thought I saw some on the kitchen counter by the sink.

(**Female**): Thanks, I didn't look there yet.

      a. He can't find them either.

      b. He'll give them to her.

    * c. He thinks he knows where they are.

She has misplaced her keys, and he suggests someplace where they might be.

**Voice 1:** Number 17.

(**Female**): Wasn't there supposed to be a basket weaving class here yesterday?

(**Male**): I heard it got cancelled because not enough people signed up for it.

    * a. There was lack of interest.

      b. The class was at a different place.

      c. The class will be later.

The class was scheduled, but since not enough people were interested, the class was not held.

**Voice 1:** Number 18.

(**Male**): Were you able to get tickets to the football game?

(**Female**): The box office said they were all sold out.

(**Male**): I may be able to pick up some extras from one of my buddies.

      a. She'll get the tickets.

    * b. He'll ask a friend for tickets.

      c. He'll give the tickets to his friend.

She couldn't buy tickets at the ticket office, but he will see if one of his friends (buddies) has some that they can use.

**Voice 1:** Number 19.

(FEMALE): Did you watch the tennis match yesterday?

(MALE): I started to, but there was a rain delay, so they've moved the finish up to today.

    a. They'll start the match today.

    b. They finished the match yesterday.

  \* c. They couldn't finish the match yesterday.

The match started yesterday, but then it rained, so the match was stopped in progress. The rest of the match will be played today.

**Voice 1:** Number 20.

(FEMALE): How's your brother's new job working out?

(MALE): Great. It's a step up from his old one.

    a. He liked the old one better.

    b. It's a lot of work.

  \* c. It's a better job.

By *working out* in this context, she means what is it like, how the brother likes it. *It's a step up* means that it is better than the old job.

**Voice 1:** Number 21.

(FEMALE): Mary's spent the last four months preparing for her entrance exams.

(MALE): What a waste of time! There's such a thing as being over-prepared.

(FEMALE): Oh, I don't know. It can't hurt.

    a. He thinks the exams are over.

  \* b. He thinks Mary studies too much.

    c. He thinks Mary isn't prepared.

They disagree about Mary's study methods. He thinks Mary works too intensely and too long. She thinks it is worth it.

**Voice 1:** Number 22.

(MALE): How's your zoology class coming along?

(FEMALE): The lectures are okay—the textbook too—but I really like the hands-on stuff in the lab best.

    a. She prefers the lectures.

  \* b. She prefers the lab work.

    c. She prefers the readings.

She likes the lectures and textbook but likes the lab work best. *Hands-on* means she can be actively involved in doing things in the lab.

**Voice 1:** Number 23.

(MALE): Whew! That was one tough exam!

(FEMALE): I'll say. There were things I didn't remember from the lectures <u>or</u> the textbook.

    a.  He did better than she did.

  * b.  She thinks it had new information.

    c.  She couldn't remember anything.

They agree that the exam was difficult. She thinks there was material in the exam that wasn't in the lectures or the textbook.

**Voice 1:** Number 24.

(FEMALE): Boy, textbooks are really expensive these days!

(MALE): I was able to save some money by reading literature texts at the library.

    a.  She didn't buy all the books.

    b.  He bought some cheaper books.

  * c.  He didn't buy some of the texts.

He saved money by using books in the library rather than buying books.

**Voice 1:** Number 25.

(FEMALE): How's the paper coming along?

(MALE): Fine, but I'd like to go over it with you before I hand it in.

  * a.  He wants her opinion of it.

    b.  He wants her to finish it.

    c.  He thinks it's taking too long.

As in Number 11, she is asking about his progress on the paper. He says he is making good progress, but that he wants to *go over* it, or examine it, with her before he gives it to the professor.

**Voice 1:** Number 26.

(MALE): I'm tired of driving. How much longer to get there?

(FEMALE) If you hadn't made that wrong turn in Booneville, we'd be there by now. As it is, we've got another two hours.

(MALE): Don't blame it on me. You told me to turn there.

    a.  He didn't follow her directions.

    b.  He wants her to drive.

  * c.  He followed her directions.

They are in a car together, and he is driving. They are arguing because he took a wrong turn. He says he made the wrong turn because she gave him the wrong directions.

**Voice 1:** Number 27.

(**Female**): What were all those sirens about last night?

(**Male**): There was a fire at our neighbor's garage. It was a total loss.

(**Female**): What a shame!

(**Male**): Fortunately, the fire didn't spread to his house.

    a. The house was burned down.

    * b. The garage was burned down.

    c. The house and garage were burned down.

The fire was confined to the garage, and the house was not burned. The garage, however, was *a total loss,* meaning it burned down completely.

**Voice 1:** Number 28.

(**Female**): Look out for that truck!

(**Male**): I see it. Just let <u>me</u> do the driving.

    a. She wants to drive.

    b. She wants him to drive.

    * c. He wants her to be quiet.

He is driving. He becomes angry when she tells him how to drive. He wants her to leave him alone while he is driving.

**Voice 1:** Number 29.

(**Male**): What do you think of the new manager, Mr. Jones?

(**Female**): He's very bright, but he's also very stuck on himself.

(**Male**): You've got a point there.

    a. They think Mr. Jones isn't smart.

    * b. They think Mr. Jones is too proud.

    c. They think Mr. Jones is not imaginative.

They evidently work together and are discussing the new manager's personality. They agree that while Mr. Jones is smart, he is also *stuck on himself,* or vain and proud.

**Voice 1:** Number 30.

(**Female**): I hear the new highway project has been delayed.

(**Male**): Yeah, it was going over budget.

    a. It will be started soon.

    * b. It cost more than expected.

    c. It will be started later.

The project was started, but then it was stopped because it was costing more than had been budgeted for it.

**Voice 1:** Number 31.

(**Female**): Do you think Joe Lyons will run for mayor? He's certainly got a lot of public support.

(**Male**): Yeah, he's expected to announce his candidacy at a news conference this afternoon.

   * a.  Lyons will probably be a candidate.
     b.  Lyons will have their support.
     c.  Lyons is the most popular candidate.

They think Lyons is popular with the public and will announce that he will run for the office.

**Voice 1:** Number 32.

(**Male**): Betty didn't leave already, did she?

(**Female**): I'm afraid she did.

   * a.  Betty is gone.
     b.  Betty is afraid to leave.
     c.  Betty is going to leave.

He asks if Betty left. The woman says Betty did leave. When she says she's *afraid*, she means she's sorry that Betty left, not that she's fearful.

**Voice 1:** Number 33.

(**Female**): Tom, would you be able to help me move these boxes?

(**Male**): I'm sorta tied up right now. Why don't you try me again in an hour or so?

     a.  He's moving now.
   * b.  He can't help her now.
     c.  He'll help for an hour.

She asks Tom for help. He says he's *tied up,* meaning he's busy now. He will probably be able to help her in about an hour.

**Voice 1:** Number 34.

(**Male**): Were you able to get any information about Mr. Arnold's flight?

(**Female**): Not really. All they'd say was that a lot of incoming flights are being rerouted because of the fog.

   * a.  They don't know when Arnold will arrive.
     b.  They know Arnold's arrival time.
     c.  They got incorrect information.

She was unable to get any detailed information, so they don't know when the flight will arrive.

**Voice 1:** Number 35.

(**Female**): How long will it take?

(**Male**): I would think it could be done in a week.

     a.  He can't do it in a week.
     b.  He did it a week ago.
   * c.  He'll probably need a week.

This sounds like a service encounter. She wants the man to give an estimate on how long it will take him to do the work for her. He estimates that it will take him a week.

**Voice 1:** In the last part of the test, you will hear a short talk, or lecture, and two short radio reports on unrelated topics. As you listen, you may take notes on the separate note page. Do not write in this test booklet. When each segment is finished, you will be asked some questions about it. You may use your notes to answer the questions.

Now you will hear a short talk about an interesting art form.

**Voice 2:**

Albert Richards is now a retired dental professor from the University of Michigan. Twenty-five years ago, he was teaching radiography (that's X-ray techniques) to U of M dental students. As he walked past a five and dime store one day, he noticed daffodils on sale for only 25 cents a dozen. He bought that bargain bunch of flowers and took it back to his lab, where it became a bigger bargain than he had imagined.

He began using radiography not just on teeth and skeletal bones, but on flowers. Over the years, he's perfected his method of X-ray photography and now has assembled a collection of more than 2,800 images of flowers (that is, X-ray radiographs). Everyday photographic film records reflected or transmitted visible light; but X-ray image results from variations in the thickness and composition of the subject. Richards' flowers look like ghostly, three-dimensional gray glass models of flowers. They appear transparent because of X-rays' unique ability to penetrate. Furthermore, X-rays yield black and white images, a medium of expression many find more challenging than color photography. Richards passes X-rays through his subject onto a piece of five by seven X-ray film, which he then uses as a negative to make his prints.

Much of his time is spent in preparation: finding the right bloom, carefully grooming and arranging it, and then waiting for it to turn to just the right alignment to suit his composition.

**Voice 1:** End of the lecture. Now you will be asked five questions about it, Problems 36 through 40. You may use any notes you have taken.

Number 36. What was Richards' original bargain, according to the lecture?
  a. radiographs of flowers
  b. a visit to a five and dime store
 * c. a bunch of daffodils
In the first paragraph, the lecturer says Richards bought a bunch of daffodils for the bargain (low) price of 25 cents for a dozen.

Number 37. What is radiography?
   a. black and white photography
 * b. X-ray photography
   c. a purely dental technique
The lecturer says Richards was teaching radiography, or X-ray techniques, to dental students.

Number 38. What does normal, everyday photographic film do?
 * a. record reflected transmitted light
   b. yield black and white images
   c. penetrate X-rays
In the second paragraph, the lecturer explains that normal photographs record *reflected or transmitted visible light.*

Number 39. How does radiography differ from normal photography?
   a. X-rays don't require light.
   b. X-rays reflect transmitted light.
 * c. X-rays penetrate the subject.
While normal photographic film *records <u>reflected</u> light,* X-rays pass <u>through</u> the object being photographed. In the second paragraph the lecturer says X-rays have a *unique ability to penetrate* and that *Richards passes X-rays through his subject.*

Number 40. What do Richards' flowers look like, as compared to normally photographed flowers?
 * a. They are transparent.
   b. They reflect light.
   c. They are black and white.
In the second paragraph, the lecturer says, *They appear transparent.* Normal photographs use reflected light and could be either color or black and white.

**Voice 1 (ANNOUNCER):** Now you will hear the first short radio report.

**Voice 1:** Our reporter, Sally Richmond, talks to a researcher who specializes in behavioral sciences.

**Voice 2 (FEMALE REPORTER):** People have always been fascinated by differences in different cultures. Today we're talking to Dr. Martin Weber, a research psychologist at the University of Michigan. Dr. Weber, I understand that you just presented a paper at a major academic conference where you reported on ways in which culture affects people's personalities.

**Voice 3 (MALE EXPERT):** Yes, you're probably aware of some cultural differences between East Asian cultures and those of America. Americans tend to be individualistic, while Asians are more group oriented.

I worked from the U.S. and a colleague worked in Japan. Together we studied 682 American and Japanese college students. We divided them into three groups and gave them questionnaires asking about their attitudes and emotions. Of the three groups, one was born and raised in the U.S., the second group was born and raised in Hokkaido, and the third group was born and lived in mainland Japan. Now Japan has four main islands. Hokkaido is the second largest, northern-most, and least developed.

Our intuition told us that Hokkaido Japanese were somehow different from mainstream, mainland Japanese. What we found might seem surprising to non-Japanese, but we think we can explain it.

We found that Group 2, the natives of Hokkaido, had attitudes about independence that are similar to the Americans—both quite different from the mainland Japanese. The U.S. and Hokkaido students valued independence, while the mainland Japanese valued cooperation and <u>inter</u>dependence. The U.S. and Hokkaido students said they were happiest as a result of their own accomplishments and efforts, while the mainland Japanese said they were happiest in society and among others.

**Voice 2 (FEMALE REPORTER):** What do you attribute this "differentness" about the Hokkaido students to?

**Voice 3 (MALE EXPERT):** Well, Hokkaido is sort of "out of the loop" culturally. It was settled primarily in the first half of the last century—the 20th century—by peasants and jobless ex-samurai warriors. We think this experience on the Japanese frontier was similar to the frontier experience when the U.S. was settled—they both developed a sort of "cowboy" mentality that valued independence, individualism, and self-reliance.

**Voice 2 (FEMALE REPORTER):** Hmm . . . that's something I never would have expected—Hokkaido Japanese cowboys! Thank you for your time, Dr. Weber, it's been a fascinating cross-cultural experience.

*Adapted from Nancy Ross-Flanigan, The University of Michigan News Service, 2007.*

**Voice 1:** Now you will hear five questions about the report, Numbers 41 through 45.

Number 41. What is given as an example of what the subjects were asked about?
    a. what they thought of their culture
  * b. what made them happy
    c. what experiences they had growing up
At the end of the first segment, the researcher says that the students said what made them happiest.

Number 42. What does the researcher say might be surprising to Westerners about his findings?
* a. that some Japanese are more like Americans than like Japanese
  b. that there is variation in Japanese culture
  c. that Japan is different from other East Asian cultures

In the middle of the first segment, the researcher says that what his intuition told him about the Hokkaido Japanese might be surprising to non-Japanese. This indicates that most non-Japanese think that Japanese are homogenous, or alike, and are all different from Westerners.

Number 43. What made the Hokkaido subjects feel good?
  a. developing new territory
  b. successful group efforts
* c. individual achievement

They agreed with the U.S. students, that they *were happiest as a result of their own accomplishments and efforts.*

Number 44. According to the report, what experience do the people of the U.S. and Hokkaido have in common?
  a. being isolated from the main culture
* b. settling undeveloped territory
  c. coming from peasant and military background

The researcher says that the experience of settling the Japanese frontier on Hokkaido was similar to the frontier experience in the United States.

Number 45. What is meant by a "cowboy mentality"?
* a. an outlook that values independence
  b. an outlook that values cooperation
  c. an outlook that values the dominant culture

Cowboys on the U.S. frontier had a similar mentality to the peasants and ex-samurai on Hokkaido: they both *valued independence, individualism, and self-reliance.*

**Voice 1:** Now you will hear the second short radio report.

**Voice 1 (ANNOUNCER):** Our reporter, Ken Sheppard, reports on studies done about the benefits of exercise.

**Voice 2 (MALE REPORTER):** We all know that exercise is good for us. We're talking today with Dr. Andrea Clark, who's been studying the effects of exercise on sedentary people, people who have jobs that require them to sit all day and who don't get out and exercise much.

**Voice 3 (FEMALE EXPERT):** My colleagues and I were interested in the effects of various levels of exercise on middle-aged, sedentary-type folks. We studied 240 people, split into four groups. We set up six-month exercise programs for three of the groups, the experimental groups. The fourth group was a control group and didn't get any exercise.

The first experimental group got a high amount of high-intensity exercise; the second group got a low to moderate amount of high-intensity exercise; and the third group got a low amount of moderate or low-intensity exercise.

The two high-intensity groups exercised on a treadmill, elliptical trainer, and stationary bicycle. The moderate intensity group just walked 30 minutes a day, and they didn't walk fast or intensely.

**Voice 2 (MALE REPORTER):** How did you measure the effects of exercise on these people?

**Voice 3 (FEMALE EXPERT):** To see the effects exercise had on their bodies, we measured cholesterol and triglycerides. High levels of cholesterol and triglycerides put people at risk of heart disease and diabetes. We measured these levels at the beginning of their exercise programs, then again after 24 hours, 5 days, and finally, 15 days after the six-month program ended.

**Voice 2 (MALE REPORTER):** So what did you find?

**Voice 3 (FEMALE EXPERT):** We know people don't always stick to their programs, so we wanted to measure how long the benefits of exercise linger. The bottom line is, we found cholesterol levels tended to improve for all three experimental groups. The control group, the one that didn't exercise at all, showed no improvement and in fact gained weight.

Perhaps the most interesting—or surprising—finding was that our experimental group 3—the moderate exercisers, who maybe just walked 30 minutes a day—dramatically lowered triglyceride levels, more so than any of the other groups. We were also amazed to see that the lower triglyceride levels for the moderate group stayed low even two weeks after the workouts ended, longer for them than for either of the two intense exercise groups.

**Voice 2 (MALE REPORTER):** So it looks like moderate exercise is not only good, but it may, in fact, be even better than more vigorous workouts.

*Adapted, with permission, from Michelle Gailun, Duke University Medical News, 2007.*

**Voice 1:** Now you will hear five questions about the report, Numbers 46 through 50.

Number 46. What, in general, were the researchers studying?
    a.  what motivates people to exercise
    b.  the effects of a sedentary life style
  * c.  the effects of different levels of exercise
The researcher says at the beginning that she was *interested in the effects of various levels of exercise* on people.

Number 47. What was surprising about the study?
    a.  The duration of the exercise did not matter.
  * b.  Moderate exercisers did better than intense exercisers.
    c.  Triglyceride levels stayed low.
At the end, the researcher says that this was the *most interesting—or surprising—finding.*

Number 48. When were cholesterol and triglyceride levels measured?
    a.  after each workout in the exercise program
    b.  during intense and then during moderate exercise
  * c.  at the start, during, and after the program ended
The researchers says the levels were measured at the beginning of the programs, after 24 hours, after 5 days, and then 15 days after the program ended, not during or after each workout.

Number 49. What is one of the things the two high-intensity groups did to exercise?
    a.  ran or walked fast on a track
    b.  alternated walking fast and slow
  * c.  rode stationary bicycles
These two groups exercised on equipment that included a treadmill, elliptical trainer, and stationary bicycle. The researcher doesn't mention their running or walking.

Number 50. What can you infer that the reporter probably expected the findings to show?
  * a.  Longer and more intense exercise is the best kind.
    b.  Moderate exercise is the best kind.
    c.  It is dangerous to stop exercising too soon.
The reporter's final comment indicates that he would have expected long, vigorous workouts to be more effective than moderate exercise.

<u>End of Practice Test 2</u>

# Part 3 (GCVR) Practice Test Keys and Commentary

**Key to and Commentary on Part 3, Practice Test 1**

**Key to Part 3, Practice Test 1**

## GRAMMAR

| | | | | |
|---|---|---|---|---|
| 1. a | 7. a | 13. b | 19. d | 25. a |
| 2. a | 8. d | 14. a | 20. a | 26. a |
| 3. d | 9. b | 15. c | 21. c | 27. b |
| 4. b | 10. c | 16. d | 22. d | 28. c |
| 5. d | 11. c | 17. b | 23. b | 29. b |
| 6. c | 12. c | 18. a | 24. d | 30. a |

## CLOZE

| | | | | |
|---|---|---|---|---|
| 31. c | 35. a | 39. d | 43. b | 47. d |
| 32. d | 36. c | 40. a | 44. a | 48. c |
| 33. b | 37. c | 41. a | 45. c | 49. b |
| 34. a | 38. c | 42. a | 46. d | 50. a |

## VOCABULARY

| | | | | |
|---|---|---|---|---|
| 51. a | 57. a | 63. b | 69. d | 75. c |
| 52. c | 58. c | 64. b | 70. d | 76. b |
| 53. b | 59. b | 65. d | 71. d | 77. d |
| 54. a | 60. d | 66. b | 72. b | 78. a |
| 55. d | 61. c | 67. b | 73. a | 79. c |
| 56. a | 62. a | 68. a | 74. a | 80. b |

## READING

| | | | | |
|---|---|---|---|---|
| 81. b | 85. b | 89. b | 93. c | 97. c |
| 82. d | 86. d | 90. b | 94. b | 98. c |
| 83. a | 87. c | 91. b | 95. d | 99. a |
| 84. a | 88. a | 92. d | 96. a | 100. b |

# Commentary on Part 3, Practice Test 1

## GRAMMAR

1. a. *Majority*, like *most* or *a lot of*, quantifies *scientists*, and *scientists* takes the plural verb form.

2. a. In the subject position, a gerund form *(locking)* is needed at the head of the clause.

3. d. Tests choice of modal verb as well as tense. Since the choice of asking for a ride was an option in the past, a past tense form of the modal verb should be used.

4. b. Tests relative clause. Can be correct with or without *which*, but relative clauses never take an additional pronoun *(it or them)*. *Afraid of* is an adjective plus a preposition and the preposition *of* can't be deleted.

5. d. The noun *failure* is modified by the adjective *constant*. *Because of* needs to be followed by a noun phrase—a noun *(failure)* plus pronoun *(his)* plus adjective *(constant)*.

6. c. *Are* requires a verb *(interested)*. *Have* would require a noun such as *interest*. *Interesting* is wrong because it is an adjective describing what the students are like rather than how they feel about art.

7. a. This is a hypothetical question (here an offer of possible help), so the *if* is needed. *What* is needed since it is a question. *As if* would be used for comparison.

8. d. The verb *seem* needs the infinitive *to be*.

9. b. This is an embedded relative clause. *What* is needed because it means "the thing that."

10. c. Tests passive voice and the adverb form *easily*.

11. c. The connector *although* should not have another connector at the beginning of the second clause, just subject plus verb clause.

12. c. Tests choice of preposition for use with the verb *trust*. Sometimes verbs often used with certain prepositions are called **two-word verbs.** It is best to memorize them as a unit.

13. b. Tests choice of modal; *must* means the speaker is certain.

14. a. *That* refers to the problem; *other than* means everything else about the cake, like *except for* or *besides*. The wrong answers b and c are nonsensical.

15. c. The verb *impressed* requires the preposition *by* or *with* in this context.

16. d. The present progressive tense is needed here. The infinitive *to guard* would also be acceptable.

17. b. The gerund *doing* is used with the two-word verb *thought of* here. A gerund or noun phrase is needed after a preposition *(of)*.

18. a. In this clause, *how* is used alone to modify *expensive*.

19. d. This tests verb choice *(have* or *do)* and past pertect tense. *Wish* plus the reference to the past make the past perfect tense necessary.

20. a. Pronouns *(it, them)* are not used at the end of relative clauses; this sentence uses active rather than passive voice.

21. c. Infinitive followed by gerund is correct here; *finish* takes the gerund.

22. d. This gerund uses the passive voice. Either a noun phrase (such as *new employment*) or a gerund *(being hired)* must be used here, following the *of*.

23. b. The adjective *quite* modifies *enough*, which in turn modifies *hot*. *Too* cannot modify *enough*.

24. d. The pronoun *them* referring to carrots is used as the object. It cannot be deleted.

25. a. A comparative *than* should be used rather than a preposition.

26. a. The word order must take the question form, and the modal *have to* requires the auxiliary verb *do*.

27. b. The infinitive of an active verb is used here. Many adjectives (such as *easy, difficult, nice,* etc.) are commonly followed by infinitives.

28. c. This adjective string tests word order used with *so*. *Such a lovely* would also be acceptable.

29. b. *Moreover* is the only connector to express addition; all the other connectors given would be used for a second phrase with a contrary or contrasting meaning.

30. a. This adverb is a negative quantifier and should be memorized much as vocabulary is.

## CLOZE

31. c. A singular noun meaning study or investigation is needed here.

32. d. A plural noun that refers to the source of the data or evidence is needed here.

33. b. An adjective modifying a plural noun is necessary.

34. a. The clause connector *that* is necessary.

35. a. A noun is needed; we know from the first sentence that this passage will concern shifts in climate.

36. c. A noun meaning a set space of time, *period* fits here.

37. c. A plural noun meaning climate or weather itself is needed here. Changes or shifts in weather do not fit.

38. c. A quantifiable noun is required. Weather, sun, and crop cannot rise and fall.

39. d. To fit here, the verb must mean the opposite of *falls*. *Ups* and *high* are not verbs, and *increase* is grammatically incorrect.

40. a. The past tense of *take* is needed here. *Was* cannot be used with *place*, and *in* is not a verb.

41. a. The pronoun *they*, which follows in the sentence, indicates that both England and Europe are being referred to.

42. a. *Than* is needed to express the contrast or change in the weather pattern.

43. b. All the other choices would make this an incomplete or run-on sentence.

44. a. A comparative adjective is needed here; *warmer* would be contradictory to the sense of the sentence.

45. c. A noun meaning an area or location is needed here.

46. d. A verb expressing belief or thought is needed here.

47. d. A noun meaning change or alteration is needed here.

48. c. This adjective locates the part of the atmosphere where the change occurred. A descriptive adjective such as *windy* does not make sense in this context.

49. b. *By* is the only preposition that goes with the two-word verb *governed by*.

50. a. A verb expressing a change is needed here. *Turn* is semantically incorrect in this context.

## VOCABULARY

51. a. Here, positive, meaning *certain,* or *sure,* can be contrasted with *uncertain* or *unsure*; positive is also the opposite of negative.

52. c. Somewhat colloquial. To *trail* someone is to follow after him or her, in his or her path or trail.

53. b. Informal but common term; it can also be used to mean to get someone's attention.

54. a. An involuntary shaking or shivering; it can be caused by excitement, fear, cold, etc.

55. d. A meeting that is unplanned or brief.

56. a. To confuse or perplex. As a noun, can mean a barrier or partition.

57. a. To be unhappy from loss of hope or confidence.

58. c. A colloquialism, meaning as fast and as easy as to *snap one's fingers*. A *snap* is a sharp, cracking sound.

59. b. Can also mean ineffective; not strong. A very old or very sick person may be *feeble,* as may a poor response or argument.

60. d. Can also mean reliable; related to the noun *creed,* a formal statement of beliefs.

61. c. To think carefully about something.

62. a. An informal term meaning to push roughly.

63. b. To be reluctant, and usually complaining; semantically related to the verb *begrudge*.

64. b. *Common* in the sense of being widespread or predominant.

65. d. Often used in the sense of taking risks or chances, as *speculators* in the stock market.

66. b. To be *ignorant of* means to not know about.

67. b. This means strong. *Muscular* would be used only for living organisms and is not appropriate for an inanimate object.

68. a. The same semantic meaning as a method. The other choices, while semantically related, are inappropriate here.

69. d. A colloquialism meaning to be able to interpret beyond what was actually written on the lines, thus to *see between the lines* of writing.

70. d. To speak very quietly and indistinctly. The wrong answer choices are unrelated to speaking.

71. d. A boundary or wall; *frontier* would be used for a geographical marker.

72. b. This means being healthy, growing well, and is often used in referring to crops.

73. a. To scatter lightly with water or rain.

74. a. Completely and without reservation or conditions.

75. c. To keep over a period of time.

76. b. Characteristics of a person or thing. *Principles* would be related to moral virtues, *functions* to uses.

77. d. To handle awkwardly and with difficulty. Sometimes people *fumble for words* when they don't know what to say.

78. a. To be slow and uncertain about a decision.

79. c. To draw the opponent's attention away; related to *diverge*, meaning to go in different directions.

80. b. Needing great energy or exertion. *Ardent* would be used to express strong feelings.

## READING

81. b. The second paragraph explains that pharmacologists and cell biologists are interested in sponges because of their chemical compounds, which may be used in drugs in the future.

82. d. In the first paragraph, the author says, *they have been around for centuries*; in other words, they have survived despite their primitive form.

83. a. In the second sentence, the author says sponges are primitive, then gives examples to justify this: lack of muscles and nerves, no mouth or digestive cavity, no organs.

84. a. In Paragraph 2, *after centuries in the bathtub* means sponges have been used for bathing, as well as for general cleaning.

85. b. The first sentence states that until the 19th century, sponges *were called zoophytes, the animal-plants.*

86. d. The passage states that *for a baby with impaired hearing, the peaks take longer [not are longer] to appear,* and that in *conductive deafness, which can be treated, wave patterns will emerge [appear or show themselves] if the intensity of the sound is increased.* Choice a would be true of untreatable deafness and choice c is true for normal infants.

87. c. The electrodes *pick up,* or detect, *the electrode activity thus evoked [stimulated] in the brain.*

88. a. *Absence of all . . . waves indicates total sensory-neural deafness, usually untreatable.* Also see item 86.

89. b. After amplification, the electrical signals are *fed into a computer and printed out. . . .*

90. b. The first sentence stresses the importance of early detection of deafness. No mention is made in the passage of accuracy or learning to administer or interpret the test.

91. b. The first paragraph tells of how 19th-century magicians used scientific inventions to produce "magic." The second paragraph uses the magician Etienne Robert to exemplify this.

92. d. The first paragraph tells that magicians used traditional skills in combination with new scientific inventions. Choices a and b would be examples of traditional skills; choice c can be ruled out because nowhere does the passage say the magicians were more intelligent than the public.

93. c. Near the end of the passage, it is stated that the images were projected onto the smoke, and that the movements of the smoke made them appear to be alive.

94. b. The passage states that *images were projected from [Robert's] concealed magic laterns.*

95. d. The entire second paragraph can be seen as an example of what is stated more generally in the first paragraph. See also item 91.

96. a. The passage states that the mushrooms become *soggy,* or filled with moisture, if steady heat is not maintained.

97. c. In the second sentence, the author states that *freezing produces erratic [unpredictable] results,* and that it depends on the species.

98. c. The brick cap is a kind of mushroom. In the third sentence, the author states that the brick cap fruits late in the fall; it is given as an example of a species that freezes well.

99. a. Here, the storage technique used (jars) is the only procedure given that will protect properly prepared mushrooms. The other choices all concern preparation of mushrooms.

100. b. At the beginning of the second paragraph, the author states that *good circulation of warm air . . . is the most important principle. Steady heat* is also stressed, but it does not appear as an answer choice.

## Key to Part 3, Practice Test 2

### GRAMMAR

| | | | | |
|---|---|---|---|---|
| 1. a | 7. a | 13. b | 19. a | 25. a |
| 2. c | 8. b | 14. a | 20. c | 26. d |
| 3. d | 9. d | 15. a | 21. a | 27. b |
| 4. d | 10. c | 16. d | 22. d | 28. c |
| 5. b | 11. a | 17. b | 23. b | 29. d |
| 6. a | 12. c | 18. c | 24. a | 30. d |

## CLOZE

| | | | | |
|---|---|---|---|---|
| 31. d | 35. c | 39. d | 43. b | 47. d |
| 32. b | 36. a | 40. a | 44. c | 48. a |
| 33. a | 37. c | 41. d | 45. b | 49. b |
| 34. c | 38. d | 42. a | 46. b | 50. d |

## VOCABULARY

| | | | | |
|---|---|---|---|---|
| 51. d | 57. b | 63. a | 69. c | 75. b |
| 52. c | 58. d | 64. b | 70. a | 76. c |
| 53. a | 59. b | 65. a | 71. b | 77. d |
| 54. b | 60. a | 66. a | 72. c | 78. b |
| 55. d | 61. a | 67. d | 73. c | 79. b |
| 56. c | 62. c | 68. d | 74. a | 80. d |

## READING

| | | | | |
|---|---|---|---|---|
| 81. c | 85. d | 89. b | 93. d | 97. d |
| 82. c | 86. d | 90. b | 94. a | 98. a |
| 83. a | 87. d | 91. d | 95. a | 99. a |
| 84. a | 88. a | 92. c | 96. b | 100. c |

## Commentary on Part 3, Practice Test 2

### GRAMMAR

1. a. The gerund form *going* is needed as the object of the preposition.

2. c. This tests word order in a subordinate phrase. *So* intensifies the adverb *often,* which modifies the verb *happens.* Each modifier should occur just before the word it modifies. *Too* cannot be used here because it is part of a subordinate phrase.

3. d. The appropriate verb tense in this context is future perfect. *By noon* lets you know it is not noon yet; later, when it is noon, the speaker will be finished.

4. d. The correct connector should express a contrary thought; all the incorrect answers express addition.

5. b. The existential *there* is necessary here.

6. a. This is a standard comparative phrase, *as . . . as. So . . . as* could also be used since the sentence is negative.

7. a. The passive form of the verb is needed here since the action will be done to the clothing, not by the clothing.

8. b. This is a noun compound, testing the form of the adjectives modifying the noun *period*. A preposition should not be included, and any plural markers would be on the noun, not the adjectives.

9. d. Often, the present progressive is used in a future context. *Will be held* would also be correct. Here the verb requires the passive voice, because the convention cannot perform the action.

10. c. The correct preposition, *between*, expresses the relationship between two people.

11. a. Here the preposition is part of a two-word verb. *Called off* means canceled. The other prepositions used with *call* have different meanings.

12. c. This tests word order in reported speech. *It was shipped* is a subordinate phrase.

13. b. *Another* can be used only for a singular noun; *other* is an adjective modifying the noun *skills* and does not need a plural marker.

14. a. This is the past tense of a passive verb.

15. a. *Which* must be included in this relative clause. *That* could also be used here.

16. d. This is the active form of the verb; *be baked* would be the correct passive form.

17. b. This tests word form *(nothing)* plus a negative connector. A comparison *(nothing than)* is inappropriate here.

18. c. This tests present perfect verb tense. The action (to know) is completed and continual.

19. a. This tests the correct adjective form for the stem *suit*. *Suiting* and *suited* are verbs, while *suitably* is an adverb.

20. c. Here two infinitives are used together. The meaning is that he had to stop (in order) to make the call, not to stop the action of calling.

21. a. An embedded verb (*let* + pronoun + *do*), rather than an infinitive (*let* + pronoun + *to do*) is needed here, and the relative pronoun (*it*) is necessary.

22. d. This tests word order in a clause; placing the preposition at the end is informal but acceptable.

23. b. The present perfect is the only acceptable tense here since the action (forgetting) is completed, and the speaker specifies the present time (now).

24. a. This is a relatively formal conditional (hypothetical) statement, using inverted word order. *If we had known*, using normal word order, would also be correct.

25. a. The gerund (*drinking*) is the object of the sentence, and expresses a continual daily action, which the speaker wishes to stop. Choices c and d are the wrong tense, and *to drink* would mean that every day the person must stop for a drink of coffee.

26. d. This calls for choice of the correct relative pronoun. *What* is an emphatic type of expression here. Choices a and b would appear in a subordinate clause, and *how* is not a pronoun.

27. b. A verb (*doing*) and gerund (*building*, meaning the action of building) appear in an embedded clause. Choices c and d use an incorrect tense, and a does not use a gerund form.

28. c. *Mostly* is a positive quantifier of the adjective *black*. It means most of the pencils are black.

29. d. For this conditional *(even if)*, *if* is necessary to show the action might happen in the future.

30. d. In questions, normal word order is inverted, so here the auxiliary verb *can* must appear first; *done* is the correct passive form of the verb.

## CLOZE

31. d. To fit here, the noun must mean the opposite of *benefit*.

32. b. A modal expressing necessity fits here.

33. a. A coordinating conjunction (connector expressing addition) is needed here.

34. c. This is the only preposition that expresses the correct meaning. *And* is not a preposition.

35. c. A connector expressing a resultant action is needed here. Choices a and b do not fit grammatically, and choice d is contradictory and illogical.

36. a. This is the only appropriate preposition. Choice d is not a preposition.

37. c. To fit here, the noun must express a thought or worry. The other choices are semantically incorrect.

38. d. A connector *(so)* is needed here to express resultant action.

39. d. An adjective meaning ideal, optimum, or proper is needed here.

40. a. An article is needed here and would precede any adjective string.

41. d. A negative quantifier is needed here.

42. a. To be semantically correct, the noun chosen must express a problem or difficulty. It refers to the *concern* in Item 37.

43. b. The noun here must express a period of time. Choice a would refer to a series of actions rather than a period of time.

44. c. The incorrect answers do not fit semantically and do not make sense.

45. b. The noun here must express the researchers' final objective.

46. b. This is the only appropriate preposition.

47. d. The verb with auxiliary is needed here; the structure is parallel *(goal is to find . . . and to be able)*.

48. a. The degree complement here *(so . . . that)* should express causality.

49. b. An infinitive is needed here. It could also take the form *in order to*.

50. d. An adjective expressing the opposite of *optimal* is needed here, to contrast *positive* with *negative*.

## VOCABULARY

51. d. This means to cover something up and hide it. Choice c, *obstruct*, means to prevent something from being done.

52. c. This means a grouping or collection of things, a total.

53. a. This is idiomatic, meaning to continue to feel angry or upset about something.

54. b. This is one meaning of the adjective. It means the person's face was red. He may have felt *giddy* (choice c), but this would not be visible to the nurse.

55. d. This means things that cannot be measured directly because they are not definite or concrete.

56. c. The manager is *estimating* or making a prediction.

57. b. This meaning of the word doesn't mean part of something. It is sometimes used in legal contexts and means to be biased in favor of something. The opposite of *partial* is *impartial*; a judge should be fair and impartial.

58. d. This means to move or act quickly.

59. b. To be *instrumental* means to serve as an instrument, or tool to get things done.

60. a. This is an idiomatic phrase used in sports. It means a series of wins (or sometimes losses).

61. a. This means to resist, or stand up against something.

62. c. This means he did it suddenly, rather than gradually.

63. a. These are groups of people within an organization that act together to achieve their goals.

64. b. *To brace* something means to reinforce it; used in this sense it means to steady oneself for a shock.

65. a. *To be sufficient* is to be enough for one's purpose.

66. a. This means compacted, or pushed together. Choice c means to make stronger, so does not fit this context.

67. d. A place where fruit trees grow. *Cultivation* refers to the process of caring for crops and *harvest* to the gathering of crops.

68. d. Something, usually a disease, that is transmitted involuntarily or *caught*. Sometimes laughter is said to be contagious. *Congenial* means friendly, *accessible* means obtainable, and *compulsory* means required.

69. c. This means to weaken and grow smaller due to lack of water.

70. a. This means the rest of it, what was left. Choices c and d would refer to small pieces or fragments.

71. b. This means visually unclear. Choice a cannot refer to a printed object, and choice c would be used with reference to a feeling of dizziness.

72. c.  This refers to his feelings about the idea. If he is *resigned to* the idea, he has accepted it, though he is not happy about it. *Destined* has to do with fate; *indulged* is incorrect because while one can indulge oneself and one's desires, one cannot indulge an idea.

73. c.  This means a bright light.

74. a.  This means having a second choice or option, something different.

75. b.  This means rough and uneven, not smooth.

76. c.  Something that cannot succeed is *futile.*

77. d.  While choices b, c, and d all mean a final result, choice d is further used more specifically, to mean an opinion that is formed or a decision that has been made.

78. b.  This means at the same time.

79. b.  This means to accept others' opinions or practices.

80. d.  This means soon, within a few moments. Choices a and b would refer to something of great importance, and choice c means with attention to small details.

## READING

81. c.  The canals are an example of a disastrous remedy; they were constructed for drainage, which was supposed to *increase food production.*

82. c.  The passage states *the canals became arms [extensions] of the sea and salt water intruded [entered] into the croplands.*

83. a.  The last sentence states that *increasing salinity [salt water] . . . threatens the nursery . . . of the . . . shrimp*; therefore too much salt in the water is bad for them (this makes choice b incorrect). They need some fresh water mixed in, so choice a is correct. Nothing is said about moving water (choice c) or the temperature of the water (choice d) as far as the shrimp are concerned.

84. a.  The salt water intrudes *in periods of drought* (when there is lack of rain).

85. d.  The passage states people thought the muck *was going to waste* (not being used), and they wanted to use it.

86. d.  At the beginning of the passage, it is stated that consumption of bakery products is increasing, and further, that baked goods as a source of carbohydrates are replacing rice and other grains. While carbohydrates (cereals) are advocated as good protein carriers, the passage states that little has so far been done in this area. (Also see Question 87.)

87. d.  The last sentence states *carbohydrates . . . are logical protein carriers.*

88. a.  The second sentence of the second paragraph states that they are now being phased out (their use is being slowly reduced and stopped).

89. b.  The second and third sentences give this information, that there is a preference for compounded bakery products and that Japan is an example of countries following this trend.

90. b. The second half of the second paragraph gives this information. India is given as an example of a country where consumption of protein-enriched bread is encouraged, and the last sentence states that cereals are logical protein carriers. (Also see Question 87.)

91. d. The third sentence states the thesis, and the second paragraph gives examples of how this is achieved.

92. c. The passage states that *fat is accumulated . . . to store the energy necessary for lactation.*

93. d. The second sentence of the second paragraph states that *nutrients [are] transported via the uterine and placental blood systems,* and the following sentence refers to these blood systems as a *lifeline.*

94. a. The passage states that *preparation for lactation . . . will take place even at the expense of fetal growth.* This means that the mother's body *thinks* lactation is more important than the baby.

95. a. The question asks what was, but is no longer believed; the second sentence of the passage states the belief.

96. b. The passage states that there was *no competent [able] architect in the colonies.*

97. d. Shadwell is referred to as Thomas Jefferson's *paternal home,* meaning it belonged to his father, Peter.

98. a. The passage states that Monticello *was developed in intermittent stages as its busy master [Thomas Jefferson] found opportunity.* This means Jefferson would work at it a while, then stop, and then work some more.

99. a. The last sentence states that Jefferson *was the first exponent in America* of the classical revival style. An *exponent* tries to promote something.

100. c. The passage states that the house was begun in 1769 and not finished until after 1809; Jefferson moved into the house in 1770, after Shadwell *had been destroyed by fire.*

# SCORING AND INTERPRETING YOUR TEST

# Scoring and Interpreting Your Test

When you take the official MELAB, all your test papers will be sent to the English Language Institute of the University of Michigan (ELI-UM) for grading. Approximately two to three weeks later, the ELI-UM will send you an official score report. The score report will tell you your final score (the average of your scores on Parts 1, 2, and 3) and your separate part scores. If instead of a final score you see **NFS**, that means **No Final Score** was assigned. This may happen if a test was invalidated, or the examinee did not attempt one of the three parts of the exam. If an oral interview was given, ratings will have been reported to ELI-UM by the local examiner, and those ratings will be given on the score report form. Oral interview ratings are on a different scale from the one used for the other parts of the test and are not averaged in with the final score. The ELI-UM will report your score to you and to any institutions (schools or universities) to whom you have asked your scores to be sent.

The scores reported are *not* the total number of problems answered correctly, nor are they percentage scores. Rather, they are scaled scores. The scaled scores are based on statistical average, or "normal" scores from past test administrations. The average score for each part (Parts 1, 2, and 3) is approximately 73–78. Here are possible score ranges and recent (2007 statistics) average scores for each part.

| Possible Score Range | Chance (Guessing) | Average (Mean) | Part of MELAB Test |
|---|---|---|---|
| 99–33 | 45 | 76 | Final (Avg. of Parts 1, 2, 3) |
| 97–53 | — | 77 | Part 1 (Composition) |
| 100–30 | 45 | 78 | Part 2 (Listening) |
| 100–15 | 40 | 73 | Part 3 (GCVR) |
| $4^+$–1 | — | $3^+$ | Oral Interview (Speaking) |

The practice tests in this book are not the same as the official MELAB, but they can give you a general idea of how you would perform on the official test. The problems in the practice test were written by actual MELAB test writers and experimentally pretested, but they were not used on actual MELAB tests.

For Part 1, the composition, you cannot really score your test yourself. You should practice writing and ask your teacher to review and criticize your work. Your teacher may use the composition descriptions and sample essays as a guide, but you and your teacher should know that only evaluators trained at the ELI-UM are qualified to grade MELAB essays.

For Part 2 (Listening) and Part 3 (Grammar, Cloze, Vocabulary, Reading), count the number of correct answers. Here is an approximation of your equated, or scaled, score on each of these two parts. Different forms of the MELAB subtests are not of the same difficulty level. The *equated* scores are meant to produce equivalent scores from tests of unequal difficulty. Therefore, *raw* scores (the number correct) needed to achieve a certain *equated* score will vary (be different depending on the form of the test).

| Part 2 No. Correct (Range) | Part 3 No. Correct (Range) | Equated, or Scaled, Score Range (Estimated) | English Proficiency Level Description |
|---|---|---|---|
| 47–50 | 90–100 | 95–100 | Comparable to educated native speakers of English |
| 43–47 | 79–89 | 90–94 | |
| 37–42 | 68–82 | 85–89 | Advanced |
| 30–38 | 60–72 | 80–84 | |
| 25–34 | 53–64 | 75–79 | Adv. Intermediate |
| 23–28 | 45–56 | 70–74 | Intermediate |
| 20–24 | 38–51 | 65–69 | Low Intermediate |
| 18–21 | 35–45 | 60–64 | Adv. Elementary |
| 15–18 | 31–37 | 55–59 | |
| 13–16 | 29–33 | 50–54 | |
| 12–13 | 26–31 | 45–49 | |
| 10–12 | 25–27 | 40–44 | |
| 5–9 | 20–24 | 35–39 | Elementary |
| 1–6 | 15–19 | 30–34 | |
| 0 | 10–14 | 25–29 | |
| 0 | 5–9 | 20–24 | |
| 0 | 0–4 | 15–19 | |

For example, suppose you answered 23 problems correctly on Listening Practice Test 1. You can see on the Part 2 range that your score of 23 could fall into the 23–28 category *or* the 20–24 category and would "equate" to either the 70–74 or the 65–69 scaled score range. Since your score of 23 is near the top of the 20–24 category, and at the bottom of the 23–28 category, you can estimate that the scaled score would be close to 69 or 70.

The ELI-UM does not make recommendations for admission based on MELAB scores. Each institution (university, college, business, or profession) sets its own standards for admission based not only on English test scores but on other factors as well. These other factors could be scores on other tests, such as the SAT®, GRE®, GMAT®, or LSAT®, or the Cambridge Syndicate or other British English and scholastic exams (O levels, A levels). The institutions also consider previous academic record and grade point average as very important. Letters of recommendation from your professors or work superiors are also considered.

Generally, the ELI-UM recommends that the institution consider your level of study (undergraduate or graduate) and your field of study. Students at the undergraduate level might need greater English language proficiency than those at the graduate level, who will be studying a field that they already know. Students studying in the social sciences and humanities fields will probably need greater English language proficiency than those studying technical fields, such as math or engineering. Students thinking of qualifying for a Ph.D. will need stronger reading and writing skills.

Different institutions (universities) have different score requirements for admission. Some programs at some schools require a score as high as 90; many institutions require a score of 85, or 80 minimum, and some institutions require 75 or as low as 70. Usually the score requirement will depend on whether or not the institution has supplemental English courses available to its students and what program the student wishes to enter.

Some institutions that have ESL programs will admit you to study in their ESL program before beginning studies in your academic field. At other institutions, you may study ESL part-time while studying part-time in your academic field.

# APPENDIXES

# APPENDIX A: MELAB PART 1 (COMPOSITION) FORM

APPENDIX A: MELAB PART 1 (COMPOSITION) FORM
## MICHIGAN ENGLISH LANGUAGE ASSESSMENT BATTERY
### PART 1: COMPOSITION

NAME (PRINT) _____ Date _____

                (family/last/surname)         (given/first name)

**SIGNATURE** _____

**INSTRUCTIONS:**

1. You will have **30 minutes** to write on <u>one</u> of the two topics printed below. If you do not write on one of these topics, your paper will not be scored. If you do not understand the topics, ask the examiner to explain or to translate them.

2. You may make an outline if you wish, but your outline will not count toward your score.

3. Write about 1 to 2 pages. Your composition will be marked down if it is extremely short. Write on both sides of the paper. Ask the examiner for more paper if you need it.

4. You will not be graded on the appearance of your paper, but your handwriting must be readable. You may change or correct your writing, but you should not copy the whole composition over.

5. Your essay will be judged on clarity and overall effectiveness, as well as on
   - topic development
   - organization
   - range, accuracy, and appropriateness of grammar and vocabulary

**TOPICS: SET--**      (CIRCLE THE LETTER OF THE TOPIC YOU CHOOSE)

  A:

  B:

**START HERE:**

# APPENDIX B: OFFICIAL MELAB COMPOSITION DESCRIPTIONS AND CODES

## MELAB Composition Global Proficiency Descriptions

**97.** Topic is richly and fully developed. Organization is appropriate and effective, and there is excellent control of connection. Flexible use of a wide range of syntactic (sentence level) structures, and accurate morphological (word forms) control. There is a wide range of appropriately used vocabulary. Spelling and punctuation appear error-free.

**93.** Topic is fully and complexly developed. Organization is well controlled and appropriate to the material, and the writing is well connected. Flexible use of a wide range of syntactic structures. Morphological control is nearly always accurate. Vocabulary is broad and appropriately used. Spelling and punctuation errors are not distracting.

**87.** Topic is well developed, with acknowledgment of its complexity. Organization is controlled and generally appropriate to the material, and there are few problems with connection. Varied syntactic structures are used with some flexibility, and there is good morphological control. Vocabulary is broad and usually used appropriately. Spelling and punctuation errors are not distracting.

**83.** Topic is generally clearly and completely developed, with at least some acknowledgment of its complexity. Organization is controlled and shows some appropriateness to the material, and connection is usually adequate. Both simple and complex syntactic structures are generally adequately used; there is adequate morphological control. Vocabulary use shows some flexibility, and is usually appropriate. Spelling and punctuation errors are sometimes distracting.

**77.** Topic is developed clearly but not completely and without acknowledging its complexity. Organization is generally controlled, while connection is sometimes absent, or unsuccessful. Both simple and complex syntactic structures are present; in some "77" essays these are cautiously and accurately used while in others there is more fluency and less accuracy. Morphological control is inconsistent. Vocabulary is adequate, but may sometimes be inappropriately used. Spelling and punctuation errors are sometimes distracting.

**73.** Topic development is present, although limited by incompleteness, lack of clarity, or lack of focus. The topic may be treated as though it has only one dimension, or only one point of view is possible. Organization is partially controlled, while connection is often absent or unsuccessful. In some "73" essays both simple and complex syntactic structures are present, but with many errors; others have accurate syntax but are very restricted in the range of language attempted. Morphological control is inconsistent. Vocabulary is sometimes inadequate and sometimes inappropriately used. Spelling and punctuation errors are sometimes distracting.

**67.** Topic development is present but restricted, and often incomplete or unclear. Organization, when apparent, is poorly controlled, and little or no connection is apparent. Simple syntactic structures dominate, with many errors; complex syntactic structures, if present, are not controlled. Lacks morphological control. Narrow and simple vocabulary usually approximates meaning but is often inappropriately used. Spelling and punctuation errors are often distracting.

**63.** Contains little sign of topic development. There is little or no organization, and no connection apparent. Simple syntactic structures are present, but with many errors; lacks morphological control. Narrow and simple vocabulary inhibits communication. Spelling and punctuation errors often cause serious interference.

**57.** Often extremely short; contains only fragmentary communication about the topic. No organization or connection is apparent. There is little syntactic or morphological control. Vocabulary is highly restricted and inaccurately used. Spelling is often indecipherable and punctuation is missing or appears random.

**53.** Extremely short, usually about 40 words or less. Communicates nothing, and is often copied directly from the prompt. There is no apparent organization or connection. There little sign of syntactic or morphological control. Vocabulary is extremely restricted and repetitively used. Spelling is often indecipherable and punctuation is missing or appears random.

**N.O.T.** N.O.T. (Not On Topic) indicates a composition *written on a topic completely different from any of those assigned;* it does not indicate that a writer has merely digressed from or misinterpreted a topic. N.O.T. compositions often appear prepared and memorized. They are not assigned scores or codes.

## Code Interpretation

Note: The codes are meant to indicate that a certain feature is *especially good or bad in comparison to the overall level of the writing.*

a    topic especially poorly or incompletely developed

b    topic especially well developed

d    organization especially uncontrolled

e    organization especially well controlled

f    connection especially poor

g    connection especially smooth

h    syntactic (sentence-level) structures especially simple

i    syntactic structures especially complex

j    syntactic structures especially uncontrolled

l    especially poor morphological (word forms) control

m    especially good morphological control

n    vocabulary especially narrow

o    vocabulary especially broad

p    vocabulary use especially inappropriate

r    spelling especially inaccurate

s    punctuation especially inaccurate

t    paragraph divisions missing or apparently random

v    question misinterpreted or not addressed

w    reduced one score level for unusual shortness

x    other (write-in: see score report)

# APPENDIX C: OFFICIAL MELAB SPEAKING TEST RATING SCALE

MICHIGAN ENGLISH LANGUAGE ASSESSMENT BATTERY

*SPEAKING TEST RATING SCALE REFERENCE SHEET*

**OVERALL SPOKEN ENGLISH DESCRIPTORS**

| Rating | |
|---|---|
| 4<br><br>4– | **EXCELLENT SPEAKER**<br>**The examinee is a highly fluent user of the language, is a very involved participant in the interaction, and employs native-like prosody, with a few hesitations in speech.**<br>The examinee takes a very interactive role in the construction of the interaction, and sustains topic development at length. Prosody is native-like though may be accented. Idiomatic, general, and specific vocabulary range is extensive. There is rarely a search for a word or an inappropriate use of a lexical item. The examinee employs complex grammatical structures, rarely making a mistake. |
| 3+<br><br>3<br><br>3– | **GOOD SPEAKER**<br>**The examinee is quite fluent and interactive but has gaps in linguistic range and control.**<br>Overall, the examinee communicates well and is quite fluent. Accent does not usually cause intelligibility problems, though there may be several occurrences of deviations from conventional pronunciation. The examinee is usually quite active in the construction of the interaction and is able to elaborate on topics. Vocabulary range is good, but lexical fillers are often employed. There are some lexical mistakes and/or lack of grammatical accuracy, usually occurring during topic elaboration. |
| 2+<br><br>2<br><br>2– | **MARGINAL/FAIR SPEAKER**<br>**Talk is quite slow and vocabulary is limited.**<br>Overall, the pace of talk is slow with numerous hesitations, pauses, and false starts, but fluency may exist on limited topics. Although talk may be highly accented, affecting intelligibility, the examinee can usually convey communicative intent. However, the discourse flow is impeded by incomplete utterances. Also, the examinee does not always understand the examiner. Vocabulary knowledge is limited; there are usually many occurrences of misused lexical items. Basic grammatical mistakes occur. |
| 1+<br><br>1 | **POOR/WEAK SPEAKER**<br>**Talk consists mainly of isolated phrases and formulaic expressions, and there are many communication breakdowns between the examiner and examinee.**<br>The examinee's abilities are insufficient for the interaction. Some basic knowledge of English exists and some limited responses to questions are supplied. Utterances may not consist of syntactic units, and it is often difficult to understand the communicative intent of the examinee. The examinee also frequently does not understand the examiner. Accent may be strong, making some of the examinee's responses unintelligible. Vocabulary is extremely limited and sparse. |

**SALIENT FEATURES**

| Speech | Fluency | rate of speech, pausing/hesitation, prosody (stress, rhythm, intonation) |
|---|---|---|
| | Intelligibility | accent, articulation, delivery |
| Interaction | Conversational Development | interactional facility (responsiveness), topic development (elaboration) |
| | Conversational Comprehension | mutual comprehension (examinee comprehensibility and examiner speech adjustment) |
| Language | Vocabulary | lexical range (general, specific, idiomatic), use of lexical fillers |
| | Grammar | utterance length, utterance complexity, syntactic control, morphology |

# APPENDIX D: OFFICIAL MELAB SCORE REPORT AND SCORE INTERPRETATIONS

# MELAB
**Unofficial Score Report: Candidate Copy**

**University of Michigan**
**English Language Institute**

---

| Last/Family Name | Given Name(s) |
| --- | --- |
| | |

**Mailing Address**

### Personal Information

Date of Birth

Sex

Native Language

Native Country

Date of Test

Test Location

Date of Report

MELABs taken

MELAB ID#

Ref #

Reported to:

## MELAB Scores

| Part 1 Composition | Part 2 Listening | Part 3 GCVR | Speaking Test (optional) | MELAB Final Score |
| --- | --- | --- | --- | --- |
| | | | | |

**Admissions Officers:** This score report is an <u>unofficial copy</u> issued to the candidate. <u>Do Not Accept This Copy</u> in lieu of an official score report sent directly from the MELAB Testing Service.

**Comments:**

**Michigan English Language Assessment Battery**
English Language Institute
Testing & Certification Division
500 East Washington Street
Ann Arbor, Michigan 48104-2028 USA
Telephone: 866.696.3522   Fax: 734.615.5686

## MELAB Score Interpretation

The MELAB is an examination whose purpose is to evaluate the advanced level English language proficiency of adult nonnative speakers of English. The MELAB is a secure test battery using multiple forms administered world-wide by the MELAB Testing Service, English Language Institute, University of Michigan. For more information see www.lsa.umich.edu/eli.

| | Purpose | Description | *Score range, mean, standard deviation, reliability, SEM |
| --- | --- | --- | --- |
| Part 1 Composition | Assessment of ability to write extended discourse and communicate in standard written English | 30-minute impromptu essay (argumentative, narrative, or expository) on one of two assigned topics written without a dictionary or other aid | 10-level rating scale: 97, 93, 87, 83, 77, 73, 67, 63, 57, 53<br>Assigned score is based on two or more raters' scores<br>Mean (average): 77.51<br>Standard Deviation: 7.08<br>Reliability Estimate: 0.88<br>Standard Error (SEM): 2.49 |
| Part 2 Listening | Assessment of ability to comprehend standard American English of male and female speakers speaking at a normal rate of delivery | 30-minute test delivered via audio recording, 50 multiple-choice test items based on short and long discourse segments including extended interviews on which notes may be taken. | Scaled scores range: 100–30<br>Chance (guessing score): 45<br>Mean (average): 78.17<br>Standard Deviation: 11.54<br>Reliability Estimate: 0.89<br>Standard Error (SEM): 3.76 |
| Part 3 GCVR | Assessment of ability to recognize appropriate grammatical forms, to recognize vocabulary appropriate to a specific context, and to understand short texts of general interest to educated adults | 75-minute test; 100 multiple-choice test items including grammar, cloze, and vocabulary items and reading comprehension items based on reading passages | Scaled scores range: 100–15<br>Chance (guessing) score: 40<br>Mean (average): 76.18<br>Standard Deviation: 14.89<br>Reliability Estimate: 0.96<br>Standard Error: 3.07 |
| Speaking Test | Assessment of ability to communicate in spoken English | 15-minute oral interview with MELAB examiner | 10-level rating scale: 4, 4-, 3+, 3, 3-, 2+, 2, 2-, 1+, 1<br>Scale level descriptions available<br>Mean (average): 3+~4- |
| MELAB Final Score | Assessment of overall English language proficiency | MELAB final score = (Part 1 + Part 2 + Part 3) ÷ 3<br>The speaking test is reported separately and does not affect the MELAB final score | Score range: 99–33<br>Mean (average): 77.30<br>Standard Deviation: 14.74<br>Reliability Estimate: 0.91<br>Standard Error (SEM): 1.47 |

*Data from test administrations in 2005. See Web site for additional descriptive statistics and reliability estimates.

Decisions regarding admission to a program should not be based solely on MELAB scores. MELAB scores reflect English language proficiency and do not necessarily predict academic success, which is determined by many additional factors. Decisions should be made in accordance with the student's field and level of study, academic background and preparation, local standards, and other relevant data. The *MELAB Technical Manual* (2003) provides comprehensive information about score interpretation (see our Web site).

# MELAB COMPOSITION DESCRIPTIONS

**97**    Topic is richly and fully developed. Flexible use of a wide range of syntactic (sentence-level) structures, accurate morphological (word forms) control. Organization is appropriate and effective, and there is excellent control of connection. There is a wide range of appropriately used vocabulary. Spelling and punctuation appear error free.

**93**    Topic is fully and complexly developed. Flexible use of a wide range of syntactic structures. Morphological control is nearly always accurate. Organization is well controlled and appropriate to the material, and the writing is well connected. Vocabulary is broad and appropriately used. Spelling and punctuation errors are not distracting.

**87**    Topic is well developed, with acknowledgment of its complexity. Varied syntactic structures are used with some flexibility, and there is good morphological control. Organization is controlled and generally appropriate to the material, and there are few problems with connection. Vocabulary is broad and usually used appropriately. Spelling and punctuation errors are not distracting.

**83**    Topic is generally clearly and completely developed, with at least some acknowledgment of its complexity. Both simple and complex syntactic structures are generally adequately used; there is adequate morphological control. Organization is controlled and shows some appropriacy to the material, and connection is usually adequate. Vocabulary use shows some flexibility, and is usually appropriate. Spelling and punctuation errors are sometimes distracting.

**77**    Topic is developed clearly but not completely and without acknowledging its complexity. Both simple and complex syntactic structures are present; in some "77" essays these are cautiously and accurately used while in others there is more fluency and less accuracy. Morphological control is inconsistent. Organization is generally controlled, while connection is sometimes absent or unsuccessful. Vocabulary is adequate, but may sometimes be inappropriately used. Spelling and punctuation errors are sometimes distracting.

**73**    Topic development is present, although limited by incompleteness, lack of clarity, or lack of focus. The topic may be treated as though it has only one dimension, or only one point of view is possible. In some "73" essays both simple and complex syntactic structures are present, but with many errors; others have accurate syntax but are very restricted in the range of language attempted. Morphological control is inconsistent. Organization is partially controlled, while connection is often absent or unsuccessful. Vocabulary is sometimes inadequate, and sometimes inappropriately used. Spelling and punctuation errors are sometimes distracting.

**67**    Topic development is present but restricted, and often incomplete or unclear. Simple syntactic structures dominate, with many errors; complex syntactic structures, if present, are not controlled. Lacks morphological control. Organization, when apparent, is poorly controlled, and little or no connection is apparent. Narrow and simple vocabulary usually approximates meaning but is often inappropriately used. Spelling and punctuation errors are often distracting.

**63**    Contains little sign of topic development. Simple syntactic structures are present, but with many errors; lacks morphological control. There is little or no organization, and no connection apparent. Narrow and simple vocabulary inhibits communication, and spelling and punctuation errors often cause serious interference.

**57**    Often extremely short; contains only fragmentary communication about the topic. There is little syntactic or morphological control, and no organization or connection are apparent. Vocabulary is highly restricted and inaccurately used. Spelling is often indecipherable and punctuation is missing or appears random.

**53**    Extremely short, usually about 40 words or less; communicates nothing, and is often copied directly from the prompt. There is little sign of syntactic or morphological control, and no apparent organization or connection. Vocabulary is extremely restricted and repetitively used. Spelling is often indecipherable and punctuation is missing or appears random.

**N.O.T.**    (Not On Topic) indicates a composition written on a topic completely different from any of those assigned; it does not indicate that a writer has merely digressed from or misinterpreted a topic. N.O.T. compositions often appear prepared and memorized. They are not assigned scores or codes.

# MELAB COMPOSITION CODES

| | | | |
|---|---|---|---|
| a | topic especially poorly or incompletely developed | m | especially good morphological control |
| b | topic especially well developed | n | vocabulary especially narrow |
| c | organization especially inappropriate to material | o | vocabulary especially broad |
| d | organization especially uncontrolled | p | vocabulary use especially inappropriate |
| e | organization especially well controlled | q | vocabulary use especially appropriate |
| f | connection especially poor | r | spelling especially inaccurate |
| g | connection especially smooth | s | punctuation especially inaccurate |
| h | syntactic (sentence level) structures especially simple | t | paragraph divisions missing or apparently random |
| i | syntactic structures especially complex | v | question misinterpreted or not addressed |
| j | syntactic structures especially uncontrolled | x | other (write-in: see score report) |
| k | syntactic structures especially controlled | | |
| l | especially poor morphological (word forms) control | | |

# APPENDIX E: ANSWER SHEETS FOR PRACTICE TESTS

# MELAB PART 2: LISTENING TEST

YOUR SIGNATURE _____

DATE _____ FORM _____

## IMPORTANT DIRECTIONS FOR MARKING ANSWERS

- Use a #2 (soft) pencil only.
- Do NOT use ink or ballpoint pens.
- Make heavy black marks that fill the circle completely.
- Erase cleanly any answer you wish to change.
- Make no stray marks on the answer sheet.
- Do not fold or crease the answer sheet.
- The examiner will tell you how to grid in the identification section.

### EXAMPLES

WRONG  1 Ⓧ ◯ ◯
WRONG  2 ◯ ⊘ ◯
WRONG  3 ◯ ◯ ◯ (dot)
RIGHT  4 ◯ ● ◯

## LISTENING

| | A B C | | A B C | | A B C | | A B C | | A B C |
|---|---|---|---|---|---|---|---|---|---|
| 1 | ◯◯◯ | 11 | ◯◯◯ | 21 | ◯◯◯ | 31 | ◯◯◯ | 41 | ◯◯◯ |
| 2 | ◯◯◯ | 12 | ◯◯◯ | 22 | ◯◯◯ | 32 | ◯◯◯ | 42 | ◯◯◯ |
| 3 | ◯◯◯ | 13 | ◯◯◯ | 23 | ◯◯◯ | 33 | ◯◯◯ | 43 | ◯◯◯ |
| 4 | ◯◯◯ | 14 | ◯◯◯ | 24 | ◯◯◯ | 34 | ◯◯◯ | 44 | ◯◯◯ |
| 5 | ◯◯◯ | 15 | ◯◯◯ | 25 | ◯◯◯ | 35 | ◯◯◯ | 45 | ◯◯◯ |
| 6 | ◯◯◯ | 16 | ◯◯◯ | 26 | ◯◯◯ | 36 | ◯◯◯ | 46 | ◯◯◯ |
| 7 | ◯◯◯ | 17 | ◯◯◯ | 27 | ◯◯◯ | 37 | ◯◯◯ | 47 | ◯◯◯ |
| 8 | ◯◯◯ | 18 | ◯◯◯ | 28 | ◯◯◯ | 38 | ◯◯◯ | 48 | ◯◯◯ |
| 9 | ◯◯◯ | 19 | ◯◯◯ | 29 | ◯◯◯ | 39 | ◯◯◯ | 49 | ◯◯◯ |
| 10 | ◯◯◯ | 20 | ◯◯◯ | 30 | ◯◯◯ | 40 | ◯◯◯ | 50 | ◯◯◯ |

Mark Reflex® forms by NCS Pearson MM246325-1     6     ED06     Printed in U.S.A.

---

## SIDE 1

### PRINT YOUR NAME IN THE BLOCKS PROVIDED, BLACKEN THE CORRESPONDING CIRCLE.

LAST NAME          FIRST          MI

FORM

A B C D E F G H I J K L M N O P Q R S T U V W X Y Z

### BIRTHDATE
DAY   YEAR
Jan Feb Mar Apr May Jun Jul Aug Sep Oct Nov Dec
0 1 2 3 4 5 6 7 8 9

### CENTER #
0 1 2 3 4 5 6 7 8 9

### ID #
0 1 2 3 4 5 6 7 8 9

### TEST DATE
DAY   YEAR
Jan Feb Mar Apr May Jun Jul Aug Sep Oct Nov Dec
0 1 2 3 4 5 6 7 8 9

SIDE 2

MELAB PART 3: GRAMMAR, CLOZE, VOCABULARY, READING

YOUR SIGNATURE

DATE

FORM

OFFICE USE ONLY